Cover photograph

The work illustrated on the cover was kindly lent by the artists below. Many thanks to Denise Hendeson, Terry McCartney and Martin Senior from the Northern Centre for Contemporary Art, Sunderland, for their assistance with the cover. Cover Photograph by Colin Cuthbert. See photo for numerical key to artists' work.

1 Glass vase by **Stuart Akroyd**, Frederick Street Studios, 52 Back Frederick Street, Sunderland SR1 1NA tel 091 510 1377

2 *The Fish Chair,* by **Keith Ashford**, 18 Derwentdale Gardens, High Heaton, Newcastle tel 091 281 2769

3 Embroided tapestry by **Julie Heppell**, 22 Mandarin Lodge, Felling, Gateshead tel 091 469 8015

4 Landscape, oil on canvas, by **Alan McGinn**, 53 Front Street, East Bolden, Tyne & Wear NE38 0SH tel 091 519 2275 (collection David Butler)

5 *Come on in out of the dark*, papier maché relief wooden box by **Cath Rives**, 3 Thornhill Gardens, Sunderland SR2 7LD tel 091 510 1820

6 *Its OK to make mistakes,* polychrome wood, by **Chris Sell**, 1 St Bedes Terrace, Sunderland SR2 8HS tel 091 565 3402 (collection Susan Jones and Richard Padwick)

7 *The end of the road,* photomontage by **Nicky Taylor**, Burn Cottage, 1 Noble Terrace, Sunderland SR2 8LX (collection Helen Smith)

Acknowledgements

Many thanks to all the artists and craftspeople and other experts who generously spent time sharing their experience of selling their work. Particular thanks to those who gave longer interviews: Jane Adam, Jonathan Andersson, Helen Bennett, Vicki Cassidy, Sheila Clarkson, Andy Christian, Michelle Farmer, Arthur Findlater, Frannie, Carmel Hayes, John Hughes, Mel Humphreys, John Hutchins, Claire Johnson, Erica Just, Morris Latham, John Leach, Gerri Morris, Wendy Shales, Ken Stradling, Lorraine Voysey, Carole Waller and Anna Warsop.

455/1

Contents

About this book 7

1   **Selling** 8
    The rewards 8
    Why is selling important? 10
    What's holding you back? 11
    Suspicion of the art market 12
    Look at your strengths 13

2   **Marketing** 15
    What is marketing? 15

3   **Making marketing work for you** 18
    Stage 1: You & your work 18
    Stage 2: The market 19
    Stage 3: Your objectives 22
    Stage 4: The action plan 23
    Stage 5: Marketing in action 24
    Stage 6: Learn from your experience 24

4   **Pricing** 25
    Calculate your costs 26
    Set the value 29
    Different prices for different purposes 31
    Which price should you quote? 33

5   **Shops & galleries** 36
    The main outlets 36
    Assessing their success 39
    How to approach galleries & shops 41
    What's the deal? 42
    Do you want their advice? 43

6   **Trade fairs & markets** 46
    Trade fairs 48
    Markets 51
    New initiatives 52

Contents

7   **Selling from house or studio 54**
 A regular or occasional event? 54
 Practical & legal considerations 57
 Promotion 60

8   **Exhibitions 61**
 Taking part in an exhibition 61
 Organise your own 62

9   **Agents: the great myth? 67**

10 **Working to commission 71**

11 **More selling opportunities 75**

12 **Selling abroad 79**

13 **Sales administration 83**
 Keeping records 83
 VAT 84
 Getting paid 88
 Chasing debts 89
 Insurance liability 91

14 **Selling contracts 93**
 Before using the contracts 93
 Which contract to use? 95
 Using the contracts 100

15 **Selling & the law 101**

16 **Effective promotion 104**
 Press 106
 Talks & demonstrations 108
 Looking after your customers 109
 Mailing lists 110

17 **Reviewing your progress 111**
 When to review? 111
 What to consider? 112

18 **Training 114**

19 **Financial assistance 117**
 Banks 117
 Regional arts boads & arts councils 118
 Programmes for under 26s 118
 Other agencies 119

20 **Contacts 121**

21 **Further reading 124**

22 **Glossary 127**

 Advertising 129

 Index 130

About this book

This is a book for all visual artists, painters, sculptors, printmakers, craftspeople and photographers who want to sell their work.

It won't tell you how to get rich quick or teach you any slippery sales techniques to beguile the buyer. What it offers is a realistic, supportive and practical approach to the business of selling.

It acknowledges the confusion and suspicion many feel when they enter the market-place and, above all, it offers positive examples of artists and makers who view selling as a vital part of what they do as a means of communication and sharing their work with a wider public, as well as a valid way of earning a living.

Selling draws on recent research into the market for contemporary visual art. There's a section which aims to take the mystery out of marketing. Understanding who might buy your work and how to promote yourself to potential purchasers are essential steps to making marketing work for you. It examines different approaches to pricing and deals with the fundamentals of sales administration and getting paid.

There's a widespread belief that art should be bought rather than sold, that attention to selling techniques somehow diminishes the work and places it in a commercial sphere with which no 'real' artist would want to associate themselves. *Selling* takes a different stance and demonstrates that, whether you make decorative silk ikat weavings, do abstract paintings on ceramics, create demanding self-portraits or make ephemeral installation pieces out of pastry or toffee, you need to take a proactive approach to selling your work.

Going out and meeting the market offers artists and makers a real opportunity to determine how and where their work is seen. It puts you more in control and can help shake off the passive dependence on established systems for selling art which in the past have held artists back. Selling your work is an active business and can be fascinating, scary, exhausting, enjoyable and frustrating. With perseverance, imagination and a degree of good luck, it can even be profitable.

1 • Selling

The rewards

"I love selling my paintings. Although it is painful to see them disappear as I don't know where they go when the gallery sells them. My work is about communication. Selling is a very necessary part of the process, a confirmation that the work means something to somebody else."

Lucy Willis, painter

"It still gives me a buzz when I see strangers wearing my work. I'm absolutely thrilled when that happens. And if they get some enjoyment from it and it speaks to them of themselves in some way, I think that's wonderful."

Jane Adam, jeweller

"For the last eight years I have made a living by making, then selling, glass and metal objects. I make because I enjoy the challenge of creating. I sell to support my family and pay the bills which are an integral part of making."

Jonathan Andersson, designer-maker

"By the end of the show I sold around two thirds of my work. I was offered another exhibition and received some commissions. The experience was thoroughly gratifying and I wouldn't hesitate to do it again."

Frances Law, artist

"Most potters collect other potters' work. Every morning I look at the line of mugs and think, 'Who shall I commune with over my coffee today?' There's an extra dimension to a hand-made object. It's unique. It carries something of its maker with it."

John Leach, potter

"I get a kick when people come up to me and say 'I really like your work, I could live with that work and I really want it.' I don't mind who buys it as long as people enjoy it and hang it on the wall."

Anna Warsop, painter & printmaker

Right: Josephine Thom, *Pastry Portraits,* pastry, greaseproof paper, 1992.

Below: *Monday, a mountain of washing,* laundry, handwritten text, starch, salt, 1993, 2mx1mx35cm. **Photo:** the artist

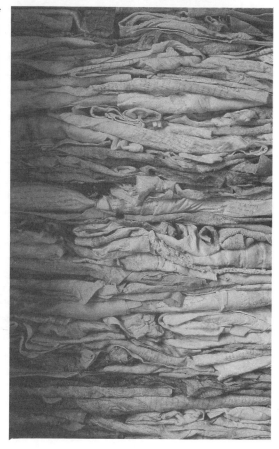

"I do installation work which is ephemeral. I work in everyday materials so I always explain to buyers that I don't know how long the work will last. I was selected for New Northern Graduates exhibition where the idea was to sell work but mine was the least saleable there.

However, I sold five pastry portraits for around £55 each to a private collector. I remade the pieces and gave the client a choice of shape, image and texture of pastry. I also had a commission for the laundry stack. It was a buyer who couldn't afford the £2500 piece I showed so I negotiated making another a fifth the size for £500. I was quite willing to reduce the size of the work to enable someone to buy it."

Why is selling important?

Most fine artists, photographers and makers want their work to be sold. In the past, artists have stood back from the business of selling. But sitting in your studio, waiting to be discovered, can be a slow and hungry process. Taking a more proactive approach offers you the freedom to determine how and where you present yourself and your work. In most situations you are the best person to sell your work. Learning to enjoy selling your work doesn't mean becoming a sharp salesperson. The starting point is talking about your work with pleasure, honesty and commitment.

There are numerous reasons for selling your work: financial gain, public recognition, pleasure from seeing others use or live with the work, contact with people, vital in what is often an isolated profession, a feeling of being part of the 'real' world by selling what you make.

Most quote financial survival as the main motivating factor. For many artists, sales make a major contribution to their income. Some are successful in living entirely from sales income.

There's a widespread recognition among artists of the enjoyment in sharing work with others. Selling work is one way of allowing access to and ownership of what might otherwise be private and exclusive.

Those who identify themselves as craftspeople or designer-makers may initially be more motivated to sell their work than fine artists. Getting known through exhibitions has always been the most desired path for fine artists with selling as a rare outcome. Makers are more likely to have received basic business training and to describe themselves as small businesses. The historical split between art and craft is perpetuated in some regions where makers but not artists are accepted onto business start-up schemes. But research into the market for contemporary visual art indicates that there are markets and buyers for fine arts as well as for crafts. The key is knowing how to reach them.

For some, selling is an intrinsic part of their artistic practice. Painter Carole Waller started making painted clothing out of a desire to see her previously two-dimensional work in movement. The clothes are exhibited in textile galleries and sell in exclusive department stores. Carole's intention as an artist is really only fulfilled when the work is sold and worn.

What's holding you back?

Don't worry if you start feeling ill-equipped for selling. Tutors at art and design colleges do little to present it as a positive option. Examine your attitudes and see how realistic they are.

Lack of confidence

All too many artists begin not knowing how and where to sell their work. Fortunately, many succeed through a combination of common sense, hard work and good luck. It's very common to experience a lack of confidence, both in your ability to sell your own work and in the likelihood of anyone wanting to buy it.

While a student at Central St Martins, Mel Humphreys was carrying a large canvas across Southampton Row for an exhibition. "A

Lucy Willis, *Her Majesty's Pleasure*, oil on canvas, 1992, 102x170cm. **Photo:** the artist

This portrait was painted while Lucy Willis was working as an artist in residence at Shepton Mallett Prison. It was awarded first prize in the BP Portrait Awards 1992. "It's 20 years since I left art school and I've been able to make a living from selling my work since 1986 when I had my first exhibition at Chris Beetles' gallery in London. He's a good dealer and represents me well. I have an annual exhibition at the gallery and he gets me illustration jobs and organises card printing for me. I produce a steady output of work. I very much like showing it and selling is part of the process."

man came rushing up to me in the middle of the traffic and said 'I must buy that painting'. I was so taken aback, I thought he was joking. It was only when I looked at his card and recognised the name (he works in the media), I realised he must be serious. I still haven't done anything about it."

Inadequate role models

At art college students are taught by lecturers who don't make their living from selling their work. They may be practising artists but their contact with the market can be quite distant. Without regular sessions from visiting artists who make and sell their work now, selling can seem a distant prospect.

The art history role models are even more unreliable. Compare the 'true' artist who remained committed to his ideals, dying poor and despised, with the impossibly rich 20th century artist whose work has become a parody of itself, obscured by marketing. There's little in either to inspire a young artist with a positive vision of selling their work.

Most artists, even recent graduates, feel that information given to them at college about how to make a living as an artist was woefully inadequate. Eleanor Newell, a ceramics student, sought advice on selling and marketing in her second year and "encountered much discouragement about considering such matters at this stage". Painter Vicki Cassidy comments, "Nobody's really prepared at art school for what it's like to deal with a gallery. The art school basically produces self-employed people but they don't tell you anything about it. I don't know why that is."

Suspicion of the art market

There's one major ideological obstacle which discourages many artists from selling their work: mistrust of the market. Like it or not, art and fine craft are promoted as 'luxury goods', command high prices and may be bought for investment purposes by wealthy people. Artists can feel the rules of the market-place subvert their intention in creating the work.

Vanilla Beer is one such artist: "The whole art system is about maintaining an elite within an elite. To be involved in that particular area of a minority within a minority is really beginning to repel me. I think that my best bet, given that I do stuff that fits into that world, is to subvert it by giving it away." Printmaker Sheila Clarkson also dislikes the gallery system: "It's to do with the fact that art is a commodity. People don't have a lot of faith in their own judgement when it comes to art. In this country people think you are an artist because you're not very good at anything

Bernard Irwin, **ceramic dish, oxidised stoneware with sgraffito, coloured with slips and oxides, 1993, 10"x11".**

Bernard has worked as an artist for 15 years across a number of disciplines: "I started as a sculptor but found I spent most of the year earning the money to finance the few weeks I could afford to spend making large-scale works. So for many years I've been a painter. But about 18 months ago I started making painted ceramics. I do abstract paintings on slab-build pots and they're selling really well. I've found that people will buy pots where they won't buy paintings. My work sells for £30 – £100 but prices are going up. I want my life to be about making art. This way I can do what I want to do. Selling my work allows me spend all my time painting and making pots."

else. They just can't understand why anybody would want to do anything if you don't make money out of it."

Look at your strengths

These inhibitions are more than compensated for by artists' positive strengths. Learning to use these to your advantage will help you sell your work, and gain other rewards in the way you view yourself as an artist.

Integrity & commitment

When you make a piece of work you know it and believe in it in a totally unique way. That integrity is unmatched in the commercial world of buying and selling. It offers the buyer a privileged view into your world and contributes to their enjoyment of the piece.

Buyers are fascinated talking to artists, seeing the view from their studio, looking at sketchbooks, observing how they handle fragile materials with confidence or use traditional tools with skill.

The close bond between the artist and the work is an essential part of what they are buying. It's what John Leach describes as "an extra dimension, one the manufactured product can never give".

Unlimited outlets

Art can be sold anywhere: park railings, smart department stores, huge trade fairs, country markets, farms, garages, surgeries, cafés and bookshops. The only limit is your imagination.

A fashionable bottled lager company in France commissioned original paintings and prints from five artists in 1992 to create a special edition of 20 beer mats for the first collection of 'Sous-Bock Art'.

A number of new approaches, often artist-led, have sprung out of the growing unwillingness of artists to rely on galleries to sell their work. Initiatives such as house and studio sales, supermarket-style art fairs and exhibitions in shopping malls have taken artists' work into new market-places. These may be more accessible to the buyers they want to reach and offer the artist greater control over presentation of their work.

Determination to succeed

All artists and makers who are successful at selling their work are driven by determination: the will to make a living out of doing what they want to do.

There's a recognition that the financial rewards may not be as great as in other professions. Hard work is involved, particularly in learning to do and enjoy all aspects of the business. One experienced maker acknowledges: "It's so difficult when you're doing everything."

Determination is also expressed in the desire to eliminate the word 'compromise' from their vocabulary. Fear of compromising their work seems to be the thing that most inhibits artists and makers from plunging wholeheartedly into selling their work. There is a real terror that contact with shops, galleries and the buying public will instantly transform their 'real' artwork into a bland landscapes or safe forms in market-friendly colours.

The reality is that artists and makers are selling challenging work within a market-place eager for pieces that express something personal and unique. Jeweller Jane Adam meets makers applying for Crafts Council Setting-Up Grants. "Some people don't even get to the stage of setting up because they are really down on the idea of actually having to sell and market their work. I think it's vital to get over this idea of the difference between compromising and responding to a challenge. It means you're trying to do what you do to the best of your ability."

2 • Marketing

What is marketing?

Marketing is not the same as selling. Marketing involves determining the needs of the customer (the potential buyer of your work) and satisfying them profitably with your product (your artwork or service).

By using marketing techniques, artists do not cancel out their right to create work which expresses something personal and vital to themselves. In fact, they are more likely to recognise the value of such work to potential buyers.

Successful marketing for artists and makers means first deciding what you want to get out of making your art (your objectives), and matching these with the market's needs, ie what the buyer wants from your artwork. A potter who chooses a working method which involves making one piece per month needs to market that work in a context which recognises its value and reflects its price. Such a context attracts the discerning buyer who appreciates and is willing to pay for the special quality of thought and workmanship which has created the piece.

The essential outcome of successful marketing is making a profit. The key to this is getting the right price for your work. Often the market determines the top price, but you must know your bottom line to ensure that selling your work remains profitable.

Artists & marketing

Marketing can be a difficult concept for artists and makers since they concentrate on making. In marketing terms, artists are product-oriented: they make what they choose to make and may subsequently consider how to sell it. The reverse is true, for example, in the marketing-oriented car industry where a new model only goes into production after endless research into the needs of a particular consumer group. It will be promoted exclusively to those people.

Marketing is often (mis)understood as making what the market wants, ie bland reproductions of safe subjects, an artist's equivalent of 'easy listening' music. But the true value of marketing is in helping artists

Erica Just, **Ikat dyed handwoven throw, worsted wool and silk, 1990, 42"x72". Photo:** Keith Tidball

"I produce a range of hand-dyed and woven pieces for interiors, using wools and silks, and I also do watercolour paintings so I've developed two different approaches to selling my work. There's a lot of time invested in the ikats and I can only produce a limited number each year. The price has to reflect that and they sell for up to £2000. But I also produce handmade cards selling for £2.40 each. They have a real purpose since they start as colour studies for the paintings and ikats. It's fascinating how people respond to different colours. With my interior pieces I've found that reds, blacks and deep greens sell well around Christmas, bright blues and yellows at spring-time. Around autumn, it's pink, purple and gold, going into reds and oranges."

to clearly identify and target their market. They can recognise that small but discerning sector of the market interested in original contemporary artwork and keen to buy. Marketing gives you the confidence to approach such groups and present your work in the right place at the right time.

Any artist taking their work out of the studio into a public context is involved in marketing to an extent. Whether seeking to sell, organise an exhibition, give a talk, run a workshop or apply for a grant, you need an awareness of the context you are taking your work into. That context is the market. With an understanding of that market, you can provide work which is appropriate in form (eg not too large or small); suitably priced (for buyer, seller and maker); well-presented (newspaper is fine for wrapping vegetables but not jewellery); and delivered on time.

Most artists and makers start with some knowledge of marketing ideas. Much of it is common sense. Painters know they can provide much larger work for an exhibition than would fit into most homes. Craftspeople know that Christmas is a good selling time, and how much people are prepared to spend on presents. Ceramicist Sally Bourne sells through Covent Garden market: "Around Christmas people have this thing in their head that presents are rounded off to about £10 – £15. They have these budgets for presents and you have to think about it. There's no point having anything on your stall for over £30." Recent research commissioned by the Arts Council in 1992 into the market for contemporary art work *(Selling the Contemporary Visual Arts* by Gerri Morris) found that "most people selected work on the basis of colour or the ability to relate to the subject matter", something many artists have observed and used in marketing their work.

Understanding the market may lead to some changes. You might begin to make decisions about the scale of work and materials used before you start a new piece. Sally says that, around Christmas, "I actually design something that will be cheap to produce so I can sell it for under a tenner". Researching how and where to present your work can avoid endless rejection and costly mistakes. It can help you value time spent making and price work appropriately.

Marketing is an active process which invites you to take control and make decisions. It won't take the risk out of being an artist but it can bring greater rewards for your effort.

3 • Making marketing work for you

A well researched marketing plan will give you a strong foundation for successfully selling your work. To develop it you must be prepared to think objectively about your work and ask yourself some searching questions. The support of a business adviser or the framework of a training seminar can be helpful. A marketing strategy forms part of your business plan and can help you gain assistance through an Enterprise Allowance scheme or raise finance from the bank.

A word of warning. Reading about devising a marketing strategy may give you the warm feeling that you have done something about selling your work. You haven't – yet! You need to work at it and put it into practice over a period of time.

Stage 1:
You & your work

Your contribution: Strengths & Weaknesses
An honest appraisal of your strengths and weaknesses is the starting point. Draw up two columns, 'Strengths' and 'Weaknesses', and review your abilities, resources, interests and personality. Approach the task positively and aim for a balanced list.

Next consider your product, ie what you make as an artist or craftsperson. Again, write down what you perceive to be its strengths and weaknesses. Try to view the work from different angles. Some points may seem mundane but it's important to list them. Under 'Strengths' you might state your painting has a particularly luminous quality in its use of colour, also that it's easy to transport.

Strengths and weaknesses relate to internal factors. Yourself as an artist and what you create are your contribution to the business of marketing your work.

External factors: Opportunities & Threats

Next look at external factors, the opportunities and threats, which influence how you take your work into the market-place. Under 'Opportunities' and 'Threats' list all those things in the outside world which affect the promotion of your work. Picture your work in the market-place and consider issues such as:

- competition from other artists, makers or importers
- the economic climate, eg as a furniture maker of commissioned work, a depressed housing market threatens your sales
- style and fashion: do they favour forms and colours present in your work?
- current issues: can affect how your imagery or materials are viewed, eg using environmentally-friendly materials.

The SWOT analysis

Having completed your four lists of Strengths, Weaknesses, Opportunities and Threats, you have achieved what in marketing jargon is known as a SWOT analysis. At this point it's helpful to look it over with someone who knows you and your work well. Expect and invite constructive criticism at this stage.

The SWOT analysis is your working drawing. How you use it is the key to successful marketing. A recognition that you work best in the evening (Strength) and hate talking to people in the morning (Weakness) may lead you to reorganise your working day. Noting that your fascination as a jeweller with crowns and regalia doesn't find favour with 1990s British buyers (Threat) may lead you to explore scope for stage design work (Opportunity). But developing a concrete marketing plan involves understanding the market in which you operate.

Stage 2:
The market

Research commissioned by the Arts Council in 1992 into the market for contemporary art work, *Selling the Contemporary Visual Arts* by Gerri Morris, shows some surprising results. These contradict popular beliefs among many artists that the public is visually illiterate and not interested in buying art. On the contrary, the potential market for original artwork is larger than imagined.

The study estimated the number of potential purchasers of contemporary visual art in the North West at around 93,000. Calculated across the UK this could mean over 800,000 potential purchasers.

Kentmere House Gallery, York run **by** Ann Petherick.

Ann offers an advisory service for buyers through the gallery, visiting people's homes and proposing a selection of work. "It's such an eye-opener. One person had a very expensive house with nothing on the walls. She's now spent several thousand pounds on original artworks and hasn't finished yet. People with no art on their walls don't know how to go about buying it. They're frightened of going into galleries, of being had and scared of what their friends will say. So you need to start with safer work. That's where prints score – they offer a first-time buyer the security of knowing someone else has got one on their wall. It reassures them that their taste and judgement are sound."

A 1991 survey *(The Omnibus Survey)* found that 11.6m people bought a craft object and 5.2m a work of art in the previous year.

What are buyers looking for?

Marketing studies find that people buy 'benefits' when they purchase goods and services. Contemporary artworks offer benefits such as colour, traditional skill, perceived value, tactile quality and creativity. They may appeal to a buyer's emotional and spiritual needs rather than basic physical wants. In order to communicate with the buyer, artists and makers need to understand what their work offers. Glass designer Sally Penn-Smith comments that, though 95% of her work is bought for decorative purposes, those buyers 'feel better' about the purchase because the work could be functional. This is important to her in the recession when people are being more careful about buying 'luxury' goods.

A key benefit of visual art and craft is its uniqueness. Any original product initially attracts those buyers sufficiently confident in their personal taste to purchase something nobody else owns. Studies of launches of new products show that these first consumers, known as 'innovators', account for 2.5% of the market. Next to buy are the 'early adopters' making up 13.5% of the market. They also want to be seen as fashion leaders but are not as eager as the 'innovators' who must have the new product first.

Avis Saltsman, *Sympathy for the bird seeking shade,* colour etching, 40x52cm.

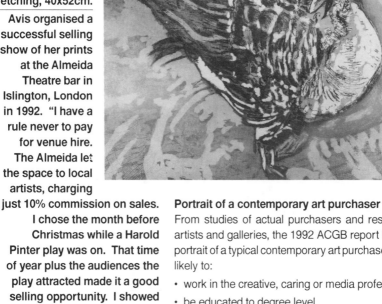

Avis organised a successful selling show of her prints at the Almeida Theatre bar in Islington, London in 1992. "I have a rule never to pay for venue hire. The Almeida let the space to local artists, charging just 10% commission on sales. I chose the month before Christmas while a Harold Pinter play was on. That time of year plus the audiences the play attracted made it a good selling opportunity. I showed work inspired by the Venice Carnival and sold a lot, priced £30 – £178. The most expensive piece sold to someone celebrating their birthday there. She saw the print and said 'I want that now'. The bar manager sorted out the sale and and the buyer took it home that evening."

Portrait of a contemporary art purchaser

From studies of actual purchasers and research with artists and galleries, the 1992 ACGB report built up the portrait of a typical contemporary art purchaser who was likely to:

• work in the creative, caring or media professions

• be educated to degree level

• have unconventional attitudes

• be, or aspire to be, a fashion leader

• be a spontaneous purchaser.

Once someone buys an original piece of art for the first time they are likely to buy again. The first hurdle is the most difficult to overcome. People buy art for unsophisticated and unexpected reasons. Artists and galleries must learn to listen to their buyers.

The report's findings on the potential market for contemporary art work were counteracted by the discovery that many galleries, shops and outlets for art did little to encourage such purchasers. In fact, in their mistaken desire to market art as the exclusive preserve of wealthy investors speaking a private language of art criticism, many galleries were positively discouraging those buyers most likely to be interested in contemporary work.

The way forward
The scene is set for artists and enlightened visual arts and crafts promoters to take a lead in marketing contemporary work. The opportunity is there to demand results from selling outlets, to use the creativity exercised in making the work to promote it, and move on from a passive reliance on galleries which has held artists back from selling their work to a wider public.

Stage 3:
Your objectives

Taking as your goal that you want to sell your work more successfully, it's time to commit yourself to sound objectives which will form the cornerstone to your marketing plan.

SMART objectives
The ground rules for these objectives are that they should be SMART:

- Specific
- Measurable
- Achievable
- Realistic
- Timed.

For instance, within the next year you might decide you want to:

- exhibit at a major craft trade fair
- find three new galleries to sell your paintings
- research the production, packaging and pricing for a new lighting concept you have designed
- produce a leaflet on your stained glass and send it to potential private and public commissioners in the UK
- enter at least six competitions or open exhibitions.

Make sure your objectives are things you really want to do, not what you think you should do. There is no point, for example, in deciding to 'export your work to France' when you have only a hazy notion of what exporting involves and always hated French at school. Your objectives need to excite, interest and motivate you. Look at how your objectives fit into your SWOT analysis. If there is a market for your work in France, this is an opportunity. Lack of knowledge about exporting is a weakness. So do you give up your objective 'export my work to France' or do you replace it with 'get information and advice on exporting'?

Stage 4:
The action plan

Now you know what you want to achieve, it's only a short step to creating your personal action plan – the strategy which plans out how to realise your objectives. Mastering one final piece of marketing jargon will help get you there.

The Four Ps: Product, Price, Place & Promotion

These four make up the 'marketing mix'. The right combination of them is essential to the successful marketing and selling of your work.

Perhaps you identify separate products or 'lines' within your work. Different decisions need to be made about pricing, sales outlets and promotion for each one.

Getting the right 'marketing mix' is not just a question of allocating the same quantity of time and resources to marketing each product. The quality of effort varies according to the importance you place on the work. For example, developing your work as an artist producing large-scale portraits to individual commission requires a longer-term approach and careful decisions on pricing and promotion, compared to continuing with the small framed landscapes you know sell well locally.

Take each of your objectives in turn and consider what you feel to be the right marketing mix for them. For instance, a jeweller who wants to find six new outlets:

- **Product**: machine-stamped earrings and brooches which can be finished by part-time assistant if orders are high. One-off pieces to be offered at a later stage if exhibition opportunity exists.

- **Price**: lower end of range: less percentage profit but work tends to sell in greater quantity. Hope orders will generate interest in one-off pieces: smaller number of sales, high prices, greater percentage profit.

- **Place**: approach up to 20 shops and galleries initially in Scotland and North East England where no current outlets. Get addresses from *Crafts* magazine and *Crafts Council Map*.

- **Promotion**: write first with slides, colour postcard, CV, trade price list and press cutting. Set up sales trip, around weekend visit to old friends. Make appointments with each shop that replies.

Making positive decisions in this way and committing yourself to a strategy helps organise your time so you can continue spending most of your time making the work. Drawing up an Action Plan gives you the framework necessary to successfully market your work without wasting resources.

Stage 5:
Marketing in action

Having considered your pricing and carried out any marketing research necessary to decide where and how to promote your product, you reach the stage at which planned marketing becomes actual sales.

The right choice of outlets for your work depends on your product, resources, interests and skills. Most artists and makers sell through a range of places, few of which remain constant throughout their working lives.

Stage 6:
Learn from your
experience

The final stage is vital. Artists and makers may feel very isolated; creating the work can be a solitary experience. Often only you can truly appreciate the rewards. Learning to pat yourself on the back is a valuable and necessary skill. Your marketing strategy should include regular review periods when you return to your SWOT analysis and your objectives and revise them in the light of your achievements.

Glass designer Sally Penn-Smith comments: "Interact – close contact with other makers (or small businesses) is a valuable asset as you can encourage and congratulate each other."

4 • Pricing

Pricing will always be a challenge for artists and makers. When you are selling in a field where the price can be so much greater than actual making costs, it's almost impossible to put a value on the intangible qualities of a work. Whistler justified the cost of a painting, which he admitted had taken only a few hours, as paying "for the knowledge of a lifetime". Until you are really well known, this argument is unlikely to carry much weight. In the meantime, you need to price your work at a level which will generate enough profit for you to survive and continue to make. There are two basic ways of working out your prices:

• calculate your costs in making the work and add a reasonable amount to cover your living expenses, or
• set a realistic market value on the work in line with what you believe people will pay.

In practice, most artists and makers evolve a method of pricing which utilises both principles. Either way can lead you to over- or under-value your work, thereby discouraging buyers. If you consistently price work too low you will not make a living out of it, and rapidly become demoralised and insolvent. Not selling anything because it's priced too high brings the same results.

Experienced artists and makers can price their work by eye, knowing the costs involved in making and recognising the special piece which has a much greater value. When you start out, ask advice and be flexible about how you price your work.

Pricing & your value

Pricing is a subjective business. Both methods involve placing a value on yourself as an artist and the work you produce. Approach it positively.

Try to view the process of pricing as estimating a work's value rather than saying "the world owes me £100 for this". If you later find it doesn't sell and suspect the price is too high you can console yourself with the fact that you value it too highly. Price your work believing in its value rather than with negative feelings of guilt and duty. Stating your

Shani Rhys James, *Red self-portrait*, 6' x 4', oil on gesso
Photo: Martin Roberts

Shani won the £10,000 Hunting/ Observer Art prize in 1993 with *Red self portrait.* **In an interview for** *Kaleidoscope* **on Radio 4, the reporter pointed out: "There are drawbacks to constant self- portraiture. For a start, who would want to buy a picture of someone else?" Shani responded: "I actually don't like selling my paintings, funnily enough. I feel very close to a lot of the paintings and, although I know it's not a professional attitude, I feel very sad when they do sell. I go through quite a lot when I paint. I can't churn them out – one painting might take me two months and to put a price on something like that is impossible."**

price with confidence is essential to successful selling and will convince the buyer of its worth.

Make sure you really want to sell a work before you price it. Anna Warsop says she likes to sell her etchings because she always retains an artist's proof. "With drawings and paintings, it's a one-off. I find it far more difficult to let go of the paintings. People always want the best ones so you're left with those you aren't satisfied with."

Calculate your costs

In the business world this is known as cost-pricing. It's a relatively straightforward way of working out the price, especially useful for makers whose work, particularly repeats or batch production, may be sold alongside other goods priced in this way.

Overheads

Add up your annual business costs that you have to pay whether you sell any work or not, eg studio/workshop rent, heating, lighting, telephone, equipment, insurance, travel, bank charges, stationery, photography, postage, accountancy, repayments of loans, maintenance and repairs, etc.

Your salary

Work out what earnings you need to live on, eg personal rent/mortgage, food, holidays, clothes etc. Ideally you want to base this on the salaries of comparable professionals. In 1993, for example, a qualified teacher's annual minimum pay was £11,200. From your desired salary, deduct regular income such as teaching fees. Take into account any Enterprise Allowance.

There can be a danger with money from 'start-up' schemes – if you allow it to subsidise your prices, you'll have to increase them when you stop receiving the start-up money.

Hourly rates

Calculate how many weeks per year and hours per week you work. Be reasonable; you might work a 60-hour week sometimes, but couldn't keep it up all year round and be productive. Allow for holidays and illness.

Work out how much time you actually spend making. You'll devote time to business matters, buying materials, delivering work, etc. None of this administration time will directly produce income. Only making produces income and it is only that making time that you can cost at an hourly rate. If, when you start, you're spending less than half your time making, you probably aren't productive enough and need to reorganise your working week.

So, once you've decided that, for example, you work 46 weeks per year, 40 hours per week and 75% of your time is spent making, you can work out your hourly rates.

- You spend 1380 hours making work per year (46 x 40 x 75%).
- With annual overheads of £3800, the hourly overhead rate is £2.75 (£3800 ÷ 1380 hours).
- On a £12,000 income, your hourly labour rate is £8.70 (£12,000 ÷ 1380 hours).
- Add the two together for your basic hourly rate for costing any job: (£2.75 + £8.70 = £11.45).

Direct costs

Add up anything directly related to making an individual work, eg materials, hire of specialist equipment or assistance, etc. When you take two hours to make a brooch, you add the direct costs to £22.90 (twice the hourly rate).

It's normal to add a small percentage (10-15%) to your total as a contingency to cover any unexpected extras. It can bring profit, give you the leeway to offer discounts for large orders or prompt payment, or cover the cost of 'rejects'. By increasing this percentage you can increase your profit. It might be appropriate to add a higher percentage for one-offs or items that sell more slowly.

This is your trade price, often known as the cost or wholesale price (note that using cost price to mean trade price is misleading – really it should be used to describe the cost of making a work excluding any profit). The selling or retail price is what the purchaser pays and includes the outlet's mark-up or commission plus VAT where applicable.

Your prices may come out impossibly high this way. If you cannot charge these prices you have to look at time (can you work longer hours or make more quickly?) and money (can you reduce your overheads or pay yourself less?). Could you earn part of your income in another way?

Textile artist Frannie describes how, when she started, she sold things at "ridiculous prices. I worked at home and had no overheads. In those days I thought it was good to produce one scarf a day, whereas now, when I'm having a day painting scarves, it's a bad day if I haven't done at least eight."

How much can you make?
If it's not appropriate to cost each piece this way, try another approach. Work out how many pieces you can realistically make and sell in a year. Divide up the annual labour and overhead costs to price the work.

Again, the resulting prices may need adjustment. Look at your expenditure and consider whether you could make and sell more work.

The bottom line
The most important thing about cost-pricing is that it establishes your bottom line. Don't be prepared to sell at a loss. It's no good creating a popular but loss-making line in an effort to make a name for yourself. You'll end up resenting making the work, and damage your reputation by turning out poor quality goods.

Michelle Bowen, Shop Manager at Cirencester Workshops often finds inexperienced makers ask her advice on pricing. "It's impossible to answer the question 'What's it worth?' I can't say that I want to sell it as cheaply as possible. Makers really need to establish their costs and know what their bottom line is."

Carole Waller, **Silk tee shirt,**
1991. Photo: Maggie Lambert
Model: Nicky Anderson

Carole is a painter whose work
takes several forms and
explores connections between
the everyday and the remote.
She paints on flat canvas,
produces work for the stage
and, most dynamically, makes
painted clothes. Each garment
is unique and signed and
carries Carole's distinctive
label 'No Walking Canvas'. "I
started making painted silk
clothing in 1987. I knew I
wanted to sell them but had no
idea of prices so I looked at
expensive clothes in upmarket
stores and priced mine
similarly. Now I sell through
Harvey Nichols, Liberty and
Harrods, in the USA and Japan
and the Victoria and Albert
Museum bought a piece for
their collection."

Set the value

The second method is known as value-pricing. For most
fine artists where cost of materials is not significant and the amount of
time spent making a work is impossible to calculate, this is the only way
to do it. In some ways it couldn't be simpler: set the price at what the
customer will pay. But few buyers will tell you what they are prepared to
pay – you have to name the price.

See 3 • Making
marketing work for
you, 'Stage 4: The
action plan'

Where do you position yourself?

Value-pricing involves researching the market and getting an instinct for
'positioning'. That is, you need to look at places where work similar to
yours is selling and note the prices. How you price your work and where
it is seen 'positions' it in the mind of the potential buyer.

Some makers have found that their work sells better at higher
prices than lower. Jane Adam had a range which she dropped because
it was taking too long to make. "Six months later I was still getting far more
orders for that than anything else so I reintroduced it, put the prices up
50% and it sold just as well."

Value-pricing involves understanding the 'benefits' sought by purchasers. They may be prepared to pay a higher price for a prestigious selling environment. A well known gallery or an open exhibition with discerning selectors can confer a 'mark of quality' on the work which a buyer values.

Pricing begins at college

Students are notoriously ill-informed about pricing. A look around the annual Fresh Art exhibition of fine art graduates shows a huge range of prices from the desperately cheap to the 'think of a number and add a few noughts' approach.

At the New Academy Gallery's annual London exhibition of 'New Northern Graduates' in 1992, the gallery had a firm pricing policy. Selector Nairi Sahakian said: "We insisted on keeping the prices low. The market is very depressed at the moment. For new graduate artists the important thing is to sell. The encouragement of a sale at this stage is far more valuable than waiting for years because your prices are too high."

Market forces

Value-pricing is not about getting as much as you can get away with. You may find you can sell one painting per year for £1500, or five for £950 each.

Be consistent about your pricing. The art market has suffered during the recession with many galleries closing. Living artists can not afford to lose the confidence and loyalty of their buyers by slashing prices. They may need to resort to marketing ploys such as giving away a drawing with every painting sold. Artist Rupert Loydell has taken to framing small work which sells for an accessible price, to protect the value of his larger works during the recession.

Printmaker Anna Warsop reports that, as the recession has hit the art market, commission rates have increased and galleries are putting pressure on artists to keep prices low. She has resisted reducing prices but has absorbed the increased commission, from 33.3% to 50% in some cases. "As a result, I now get less money than I did four years ago when I sell a print."

The real price

With value-pricing you set the price at what you believe the market will accept. Don't forget this is the retail or selling price.

You need to work down from that, deducting commission (and VAT where applicable) to reach the price at which you sell the work to shops and galleries; in other words, the trade price. Always make sure you know exactly what you will receive if a work sells.

Tony Foster, *Rainforest, La Selva, Costa Rica*, February 1991, watercolour, 22½"x35".
Photo: the artist

Tony has developed a particular relationship with landscape working on long-term projects in remote places. During 1991-2 he spent many months in the Costa Rican rainforest creating a series of rich and complex works *Rainforest Diaries*. By including in the price of each painting the cost of an area of rainforest, Tony maintains his commitment to the environment in which he worked and enables the Monteverde Conservation League to purchase forest to add to their protected area. In addition, a US company produced a series of six high quality posters from his paintings. As a condition of the deal, the firm supplied Tony with 100 free copies of each. These are sold in the UK to raise funds for local conservation projects. Tony Foster makes a living as an artist by selling his paintings, mostly in America. He feels his working relationship with the landscape is sustained by finding additional ways of preserving that environment through sales of work.

Different prices for different purposes

Once you have worked out your prices you'll find different selling situations require different prices.

Trade and retail prices

The most important difference is between trade prices (what the shop/gallery pays you) and retail prices (what the customer pays the shop). The difference between the two is the mark-up or commission which the shop or gallery needs to charge to cover its own costs. This ranges from 25% for a small craft shop to 200% for a prestigious design gallery. The shop adds VAT where appropriate so the retail price is often more than double the trade price. Note that none of the figures in this chapter includes VAT. This is just to keep the examples simple. VAT is dealt with in chapter 13.

Commission is applied in different ways according to where you sell. Fine artists selling through galleries, and craftspeople retailing through shops, have a different understanding of the mark-up system.

Jonathan Andersson, Glass and metal bowl

"For me, the only way of pricing work is to look at what the market can bear. It's a good idea to find someone at a trade show whose work you like and ask their advice. I did Ob'Art, a Paris show, in 1992 and French exhibitors around me thought my pricing was all wrong so I let them do it. They knew what objects and designs carry a premium in that market – they priced some of the work less than I usually sell it for but most of it was a lot higher. Their advice was very valuable as they knew the French market better than I did."

On the whole, a fine art gallery will take work on sale or return (consignment) and deduct a commission of between 25% and 60% (+VAT) from the retail price. The commission rate varies according to the prestige of the gallery.

Makers selling work through craft shops, shop-galleries and department stores are generally quoted a commission rate of around 50%-150% (+VAT) which is added to the trade price (often known as 'mark-up'). Again the commission varies with the prestige of the outlet. Two different rates are often quoted depending on whether work is on sale or return (eg 70%) or bought for resale (eg 110%).

There is some crossover between these two systems. For example, printmakers sell through craft outlets and studio glass is sold in fine art galleries. It is also the case that some galleries apply the commission to retail and some to trade prices. There are two important principles for artists: know how much you will receive if the work sells, and understand the implications of quoting either trade or retail prices.

Which price should you quote?

This depends whether you want to determine the amount you receive or the price the customer is charged. Some flexibility is usually necessary, if only to allow for prices to be rounded up or down. On the whole, when you are starting out you are more concerned with what you will receive (the trade price). Once you have an established reputation and are selling through more prestigious outlets, you need to maintain consistent prices and will want to exercise control over the retail price.

Artist quotes trade price

When you quote trade prices the amount you receive remains constant but the retail price changes according to how the mark-up is applied.

Example A

Trade price/ artist receives £100.00
Shop adds 40% to trade price £40.00
Retail price/ customer pays £140.00
(Retail price = 140% of trade price)

Example B

Trade price/ artist receives £100.00
Shop deducts 40% from retail price £66.67
Retail price/ customer pays £166.67
(Trade price = 60% of the retail price)

Artist quotes retail price

Where artists (usually makers and printmakers) sell through outlets with different mark-ups, some want to control the retail price so that work sells at consistent prices. You'll end up receiving different amounts depending on where work sells, but it should even itself out. Controlling the retail price is a good idea within a small geographical area but it's not always sound marketing. Outlets attract different customers and offer varying 'benefits' in terms of prestige, location and style.

Example C

Retail price/ customer pays £100.00
Shop adds 40% to trade price £28.57
Trade price/ artist receives £71.43
(Retail price = 140% trade price)

Example D

Retail price/ customer pays £100.00

Shop deducts 40% from retail price £40.00

Trade price/ artist receives £60.00

(Trade price = 60% of retail price)

If you do a lot of direct selling, eg at trade fairs, markets or from the studio, always charge the retail price (trade plus appropriate commission). It's a mistake to undercut prices in the galleries and shops you need to sell your work. Artists, often with fewer regular outlets to sell their work, seem less inclined to charge the full commission on studio sales. They should nevertheless add a percentage to cover time spent selling, organising framing and delivering work.

Discounts

With repeat pieces such as jewellery or ceramics, you can encourage larger orders by offering a small percentage discount for orders in excess of a certain amount, eg 5% on orders over £500. Alternatively, you can produce a discount price list where an item sells at a progressively reduced price when ordered in quantity, eg 1-6 jugs @ £10 each, 7-15 jugs @ £9 each. With the latter method, check prices carefully around the discount point where it's all too easy to offer more items for less money. Discounts of around 5% are sometimes offered for proforma (advance) payment.

As a fine artist, where there is a market for a quantity of your work, you can negotiate discounted prices. Printmakers have sold half an edition to organisations who provide artworks to businesses at an agreed price of around 60-80% of the normal selling price.

Sometimes a gallery suggests pricing a work 10% higher than you propose, which enables it to negotiate a similar discount with a customer to secure a sale. Haggling over prices is normal practice in some galleries and becomes more common during a recession.

Export price lists

Pricing work for overseas sales can include additional overheads such as transport costs, higher phone charges, translation of publicity materials and export documentation.

But it can be more straightforward. Glassmaker Jonathan Andersson always quotes prices 'ex-works', ie excluding all transport, insurance, documentation and duties.

If you are direct selling abroad, you need to quote prices in the local currency. But with businesses it's usually acceptable to deal in sterling. Glassmaker Sally Penn-Smith exports to buyers around the world and always trades in sterling.

Is the price clear?

A final plea to artists and makers is to approach the market honestly and make your prices clearly visible.

See 11 • More selling opportunities, 'Magazines & directories'

Research into the market for contemporary visual art has found people are more likely to buy art when it is presented in an accessible way similar to the marketing of other goods they already buy. It's reassuring to see the price label, to understand whether it means framed or unframed and to know, as in a supermarket, how much it costs. When Portcullis Gallery first opened in Gateshead, work in the shop window was not priced as it tended to be the most expensive. After a few enquiries whether it was 'possible' to purchase work, they realised this was the wrong approach. Now all items are boldly priced and sales increased accordingly.

Round up your prices in line with those in the sales outlet. Otherwise prices look very peculiar, as in the first Art for Sale catalogue, eg £4476.19 and £1248.46.

When displaying your work at a craft trade fair, having no obvious prices can discourage the purchaser who feels that asking the price may overcommit them. Lifting fragile glass and ceramics to see the tiny label on the base is fraught with anxiety. Some confident makers find that invisible prices draw potential buyers into conversation and encourage sales but this is not generally the case.

Remember that the buyer who needs most encouragement is one who has never bought your work before and may well be nervous about how much it costs. Start by being open about the price.

5 • Shops & galleries

Professional outlets offer the committed selling environment that artists, photographers and makers need to reach a wider public.

Traditionally a line is drawn between private, 'commercial' galleries and shops, and public or subsidised galleries. However, distinctions are becoming blurred. Private galleries can have hidden subsidies and may be less successful at selling than the craft shop in a public gallery whose profits support the exhibition programme. Some subsidised galleries now charge higher commissions than the commercial sector.

What is required is sales outlets with persuasive, motivated staff who believe the artist or maker's work offers their customers what they are looking for.

The main outlets

Finding outlets is not difficult. For makers, *Crafts* magazine listings and the *Crafts Council Map* of selected shops in England and Wales are invaluable. Some selected galleries sell paintings, prints and sculpture. The *Directory of Exhibition Spaces* details 1665 UK galleries. *Artists Newsletter* and other magazines feature current exhibition listings and advertisements. Many regional Arts Boards and Arts Councils have lists of galleries and shops in their area.

Craft & fine art shop-galleries

These operate with varying degrees of commercial success and artistic integrity. Easily approached, these are principally shops but may have adjoining gallery space, display areas or workshops, often grant-assisted.

A Crafts Council selected shop offers a mark of quality and you can expect your work to be displayed alongside well-made pieces by known makers, enhancing its value and 'positioning' it highly in the eye of the customer. Shops apparently distant from likely purchasers of

Collective Gallery
View of exhibition
gallery.

Alongside the exhibition programme, Edinburgh's Collective Gallery is taking an innovative approach to selling. Its new shop, Gallery 3, is stocked with small-scale fine art work in an ever-changing accessible display. A focal point is a wall of pigeon-holes, each around 18" square, housing individual artists' work, perhaps a small sculpture, a folder of mounted prints, a framed painting. Customers are encouraged to browse, to touch work and view it closely. The idea came from observing the accessible way in which artists sell their work in Eastern Europe.

contemporary work, such as the Model House in the village of Llantrisant, South Wales, can be good selling outlets. The most remote shops and galleries, when promoted through the *Crafts Map*, attract a regular stream of visitors.

Groups of artists and makers run shops themselves, controlling the selection, presentation and profit-sharing. The Makers Guild sell members' work only in their busy central Cardiff shop. Most members spend a day per month in the shop and find the contact with customers beneficial to their work. Contemporary Ceramics in Carnaby Street has traded for 32 years as a co-operative, selling and exhibiting work by Craft Potters Association members.

Certain disciplines demand specialist outlets. The Original Print Shop at Glasgow Print Studio attracts buyers with its wide selection, knowledgeable staff and changing exhibition programme. It offers customers a complete package including framing, delivery, installation and technical advice.

Privately-run shops not listed or recommended in artists' publications vary enormously in quality and ideally should be visited before committing yourself to selling there. Many are excellent but may be poorly located. Others offer high street positions but inconsistent selection process places highly-priced work alongside cheap imported gifts.

Commercial galleries

Commercial galleries must also sell to survive. Run on private money, they can't afford to show work which doesn't appeal to their customers. Their markets are specialised and range from the internationally renowned showing major artists to the small town gift-market gallery.

37

Private galleries see a lot of work and new artists will find themselves in competition with others for the owner's attention. A good gallery needs sound commercial instincts and should know its customers well. Expect a quick and honest opinion about whether your work is 'right' for the gallery, ie whether it will sell there.

Unlike the highly-publicised exclusive contracts offered to big names, most artists need a number of galleries to carry their work. When you are establishing yourself there are advantages to this. Galleries will only take you on exclusive contract if they know they can sell just about everything you do. If the work doesn't sell, the pressure is much greater for both gallery and artist when under contract.

Artists should aspire to deal with galleries showing work they like, know or respect. They need to trust the gallery to represent them accurately and to pay efficiently when work sells.

Public museums & galleries

Publicly-funded galleries, both local authority and independent, may run their own craft or fine art shop. These range in scale from the well-run Nottingham Castle Museum Shop to a small display in an arts centre. Such shops generally operate on commercial lines and may favour showing local work.

Apart from exhibitions, many public galleries do try to sell artists' work. There may be a print bin in the museum shop or space for selling work on the café walls. Artists must assess the viability of such selling opportunities. The appeal may be that they are cheap (free space and low commission on sales) and in an apparently prestigious arts venue attracting the right people. But marketing is often inadequate or non-existent and staff are neither skilled nor motivated in actually selling work. The local museum café might be a popular place for coffee but may not be perceived as somewhere to buy a painting.

However, selling opportunities through public museums and galleries are growing. The ACGB report *Selling the Contemporary Visual Arts* highlighted Artlink in Stockport Art Gallery, an innovative scheme encouraging the public to take contemporary art into their home and workplace through a loan scheme. For a modest annual fee, members can borrow artworks for up to eight weeks and then either return or purchase them. Such schemes need further development with particular attention to what they offer participating artists and makers.

Since selling may be a new activity for many public galleries, artists and makers may want to offer their experience of selling. For example, a printmaker might provide a hand-out describing print processes and edition numbering so that the public, and sales staff, understand the difference between her etchings and the machine-printed posters in the shop.

There is a need to move rapidly forward from a position where the ACGB report found "sales feature as a bonus, or sometimes a nuisance, for which the gallery is administratively ill-prepared". Public galleries should recognise that selling artists' work is "a worthwhile objective with the rewards of increasing earned income for the gallery, assisting artists in making a living and increasing the numbers of private patrons".

Department stores

Some makers, printmakers and other visual artists sell their work through major department stores. Here you will encounter the truly professional selling environment.

Your contact will be with the Buyer, maybe in the Fashion, Gift or Interiors Department. Time is money so don't expect them to be interested in the subtleties of your development as an artist. A trained eye quickly tells them, and you, whether your work will sell there.

As with a commercial gallery, work displayed costs money and is expected to sell, or 'perform'. If it doesn't it may be unceremoniously removed or put on the Sale rack.

The British Crafts Room at Liberty's is packed with small-scale decorative work. It knows its market and provides an artist's CV with every object sold. Sales have steadily increased, even during the recession.

Assessing their success

Finding outlets to successfully sell your work is harder. In a buyer's market where more art and craft work is made than could possibly be sold through existing outlets, you may feel initially you can't be too particular. But it's essential to retain some control and choice. Achieving your goals through strategic marketing involves careful attention to 'place'. Some selling outlets are better than others.

Questions to ask

Visit a local shop or gallery which sells your work, or where you want to sell. Get a feel for the place: is it busy, well-lit, inviting, friendly? Are prices in line with yours? Are they visible or does it look like a non-selling exhibition? Look at the layout: does it draw you in? Is the window display attractive? Does it change frequently or show the same pieces for months? Do they encourage purchasers by taking credit cards? Are

Victoria Cassidy, *Leo*,
watercolour, 18"x24"

Vicki is a painter working at
WASPS studios in Glasgow.
"After a year out of college I
realised I had to widen my
network of sales. I had a
coloured card printed and sent
it with my CV to around 40
selected London galleries. I
said I'd be in London between
certain dates and to let me
know if they were interested in
seeing my work. Six or seven
letters came back – I thought
that was a good return. I made
appointments and was quite
nervous when I went to see
them. Often the only
experience you've had of
people looking at your work is
at art school and tutors can be
quite judgemental. But I found
nobody was ever rude, and if
they made a comment, it was
usually a positive one. I now
have four galleries in London
selling my work."

there special credit facilities such as art loans? Do people
pass by without a glance or drop in with interest?

Do they sell – and pay?

Ideally you should visit and assess all your sales outlets
this way. It will give you a feel for the customers, outlets
and competition for your work.

An important question here is not just: "Can they
sell my work?" but, "How will they sell my work?" Remember the
customer will associate your work and therefore you with that shop, and
if they get treated badly that could reflect on your work.

But visiting a shop or gallery isn't always possible. You can't
make the work and be a travelling salesperson. You can however get a
lot of information at a distance. Get a feel for its selling style through
conversation with the owner or buyer. Talk to artists who sell there to
confirm its track record in selling and payment. If you suspect a shop or
gallery has a dodgy payment record, get a second opinion preferably
from another artist currently selling there. If confirmed, don't deal with
them, it isn't worth it.

How to approach galleries & shops

Your sales package

Make a checklist of what you need to provide. This includes visual material (slides or photographs of current work, clearly labelled); your range with details of sizes and materials, background information (CV) and prices (either indicate the range or send trade price list). If you can add a colour postcard or leaflet and business card, so much the better. Don't, under any circumstances, expect anyone to pay for this package. Present it in a folder with a stamped addressed envelope and there's a good chance it will eventually be returned. When you are getting this package together try putting yourself in the position of the gallery/shop owner. Then ask: "How would I react if I received this? What does it tell me? Does it excite me, interest me?"

Good presentation is essential and the quality of your visual material should reflect your work. John Hughes Director of Model House Craft and Design Centre describes the poor standard of photographs as "the biggest cold selling problem of all. I would never select work purely from photographs but I would certainly reject it on that basis". Some shops and galleries make an annual selection. Inadequate visuals will prevent you approaching them for another year and with some shops or galleries you never get a second chance.

Once you have identified which shops and galleries to contact, send your sales package with a short covering letter. Get the name and title of the owner or buyer by phone and address the letter personally (on a bad day, 'Dear Sir or Madam' letters can go straight in the bin). Indicate whether and when you are available to meet them to show your work.

Jeweller Julie Sellars started out by organising four selling trips to visit shops selected from the Crafts Council map. "I made appointments in advance and showed them my work. I had a really good response. In fact I got more orders that way than through trade shows."

If dealing by post, you may be asked for samples. Depending on the value of the work, some makers provide these free, others on payment. Be wary of providing free samples. Be methodical in your record-keeping. A system of large index cards with details of shops contacted, the date and what you sent them helps keep track.

Never turn up at a shop or gallery without an appointment and when given one, be punctual. Ann Petherick has run two galleries in York. "Artists were always coming in with their portfolios on busy Saturdays wanting to show me their work. They had no appointment and no idea what sort of work the gallery showed. If you want the gallery to treat you as a professional, you've got to behave like one." A painter should bring a selective portfolio of current work, a potter would present examples from their range. You may be asked to leave your work and collect it later. Smaller outlets and galleries usually want to meet you.

A commercial outlet deciding not to sell your work may be prepared to discuss why. Don't forget they aren't rejecting you as an artist, your work is just not saleable there. Ask why not and whether they can suggest any other galleries or shops to contact.

How selling outlets find you

see 3 • Making marketing work for you In some cases, the gallery or shop will approach you. Part of your marketing strategy should be bringing yourself to the attention of shop buyers and dealers. Getting orders this way helps build your confidence and reputation.

Don't imagine that once you have a certain number of outlets you just sit back and make the work. As designer-maker Frannie says: "I always assumed that you'd get clients or buyers and you'd keep them and add to them. But every year it changes. I think you have to work hard to keep regular customers."

Buyers from shops, galleries and department stores visit the main craft trade fairs. Some makers take the majority of their orders here. Reach those buyers who don't see the show with a prominent entry in the catalogue, preferably with a photograph. Use your mailing list to invite former and potential buyers. Gallery directors view mixed exhibitions looking for new artists. Degree shows are popular, particularly those in London. Get involved in the publicity and make sure anyone interested in your work is invited.

What's the deal?

When buyers place an order they either buy work outright or take it on sale or return. Both involve a contractual agreement and conditions vary with each so find out what the deal is. Commission rate is not necessarily the most important consideration. It affects the retail price but, if you quote trade prices, it doesn't directly alter what you receive. A shop may request exclusivity within a geographical area. Make sure it's the best outlet there for your work before agreeing.

Outright purchase

This is the ideal arrangement, although it's becoming rarer. Sales commission is higher on bought work than on sale or return, increasing the retail price. Payment terms may be proforma (in advance), invoiced with an agreed credit period or by instalments.

Proforma is the norm for first orders from new customers. You receive payment in advance of sale to a customer but, when cashflow is tight, proforma invoices are not always a priority.

Some makers insist on doing all their business through straight sales. Glassmaker Jonathan Andersson is against the gallery system of sale or return and always requests cash on delivery. But it's worth noting that some outlets, both high-profile and small-scale, never buy work outright and you limit your selling opportunities by rejecting them.

Sale or return

see 14 • Selling contracts

This is also known as consignment. You leave work with a gallery or shop and if the work is unsold you take it back. Use a sale or return contract since questions of ownership and compensation are raised if work is lost, damaged or stolen. Sale or return is common for makers, especially at the higher price end and is the norm for most fine artists.

The lower commission keeps retail prices down. At Cirencester Workshops, two jewellers insist on work being on sale or return: when prices are lower they sell more. Payment is normally guaranteed by a certain date following sales. If work doesn't sell, expect the outlet to request collection or substitution. Don't be afraid to suggest it yourself. Most shops feel it is their responsibility to display sale or return work. By contrast, galleries with their limited exhibition space often keep artists' work in the stock room or plan chest.

Do you want their advice?

When you enter into a business relationship with a shop or gallery, they may offer guidance on what work sells. Such advice can be beneficial, insulting or incomprehensible. Try to listen to it with an open mind. The buyer or gallery owner is sharing their commercial expertise with you. You should equally share your expertise with them. After all, if you have been selling work for a while, you are the person who knows what has worked elsewhere (eg pricing or presentation). That advice may not be suitable for a particular gallery or shop but you don't know until you discuss it with them. Listening to and acknowledging their advice, and contributing your knowledge (and expecting that to be acknowledged) establishes a professional relationship and creates mutual respect.

Price

Guidance from a shop or gallery can be useful. A shop saying they can sell your earrings at £25 but not £28 may have an accurate idea of the market. Be flexible but businesslike. Artists are wise to be wary of galleries who, in good times, want to price your work high (to get higher commission) and, in a recession, want to price it low (to get more sales).

The work

You may find it more difficult to receive advice on your work. A ceramicist complained about a shop buyer who only wanted her to produce blue coffee sets. "I can't understand it. He seems to be totally wrapped up in selling. He just wants me to do things that sell."

Artist Anna Warsop did a series of white abstract paintings which sold well: "I've had galleries say 'We can sell any number of these white paintings because they go with magnolia walls'. I then started doing black paintings and was dropped – they didn't go with magnolia walls and the galleries didn't like the style. But with white paintings, I came to a point where I had exhausted what I wanted to do with them. You knew you were painting pound notes so you couldn't actually do it."

The approach to makers and artists seems to be different. Shops often view makers' work as a product and expect constant new lines. Subtle changes of influence and form are not generally appreciated. Galleries want artists' work to be consistent and see it as a sales risk if style, content, form and materials alter. Don't let their advice inhibit the development of your work.

Sue Dunkley found, after many years of selling through London galleries and with three sell-out shows to her credit, that "the pressures and strains of compromise in working with a gallery were impairing my work as an artist. I decided to pull out to explore my imagery and have spent seven years selling through studio sales. Now I've reached the point where I'm ready to go back into the system. I'm more confident and articulate now, I need to be seen and to get the right prices for my work. I've gone back to my original gallery and have a big show coming up. Galleries and artists need each other. They should have a real trust in each other."

Presentation

Advice on how to best frame your work can be helpful, although beware of bulk-buying framing materials since styles change. Special packaging may enhance the price your work commands.

Selling through shops and galleries

ADVANTAGES
• Accessible, easily identified outlets.
• Professional outlets sell work leaving you time to make it.
• Indirect selling method avoiding face-to-face contact with customers.
• Large orders with some outlets.
• Buyer/owner assesses saleability increasing likelihood of sales.

DISADVANTAGES
• Dependent on others to represent and display your work.
• Not meeting customers gives limited feedback.
• May not be able to get purchasers' names for your own promotion.
• Sale or return can work to your disadvantage.
• Payment may be slow.

6 • Trade fairs & markets

Selling through trade fairs, markets and festivals are popular methods of direct selling. You display your work and meet the customer in person. They are great places to get the experience you need to confidently sell your work.

Which fair or market?

Selecting the right one for you is important. Commercial success or failure cannot always be predicted but research will help you decide.

Certain trade fairs and markets have an established track record. Ask around for recommendations. RABs and the Crafts Council produce listings; the Rural Crafts Association provides members with details of major country fairs; Write Angle Press publish *The Craftworker's Yearbook*, a comprehensive directory of national craft fairs. Look out for art fairs in *Artists Newsletter* listings.

New initiatives may not offer a track record but enthusiasm and inspired marketing can make a fresh approach successful. The Country Living Fair, held for the first time in recession-hit 1992 London, was a huge success for many exhibitors. Ceramicist Mike Francis reported his best two days selling in twelve years. Also in 1992, Collective Gallery in Edinburgh organised a pre-Christmas 'Alternative Art Mart'. With 1000 works for sale by 100 artists at prices from £5 – £1500, plenty was sold, mostly priced around £50. Gallery Director Cindy Sughrue said: "People don't realise they can buy an original work by a young artist for the price of a Habitat poster. We'd certainly repeat the Art Mart and see it a way of helping artists sell their work and encouraging new visitors to the gallery. We took 33% commission on sales and broke even this year. With more publicity, we might even make a small profit to help promote the gallery's exhibition programme."

Look at the promotion

With an annual event ask the organisers for the previous year's catalogue plus sales and attendance figures if available. Is your work compatible? How professional is the marketing? Compare sales and attendance figures with other events? Contact previous exhibitors for their experience.

What will it cost you?

see 4 • Pricing

Exhibiting at a local fair or market may be your first major outlay on promotion. You need to calculate your costs and be reasonably confident of covering these through sales.

Expenditure may include travel, accommodation and subsistence; paying an assistant to cover the workshop or help at the fair; display shelving or cases (recoup the costs over several fairs); insurance; making and tying up stock; credit card arrangements; telephone; lighting; and publicity material. Don't forget to cost in lost production time. As you become more experienced you can develop new ways of covering your costs. Sally Penn-Smith exhibited at Lifestyle Europe, a major Tokyo trade fair in 1993. She advertised in *Artists Newsletter* for designer-makers interested in marketing their work in Japan and, for a fee, offered to represent their work through a portfolio and distribution of price lists and cards.

Stands are hired according to size and facilities. Work out how much space you can afford. Sharing a stand may be a solution but make sure you won't be in direct competition with each other. Check the position: newcomers are often fobbed off with space that is hard to let. Good lighting is important and worth paying for. At the Business Design Centre's artMart there was a clear distinction between larger well-lit stands and tiny dimly-lit booths.

With experience of major international trade fairs, glassmaker Jonathan Andersson reckons the greatest impact could be made with a group stand representing four or five makers. "A large, well-lit, beautifully designed stand would draw buyers in like a shop or gallery and be so much more attractive than an individual booth." But the organisation of a group stand is not always straightforward.

Tony Warner took a group stand at the Business Design Centre's ART 90 fair. He described sales as reasonable: "Some artists did very well and anybody who sold anything more than got their money back" but organisation was a problem: "Artists helped when they could, resulting in one person on the stand at one time and eight at another! When customers revisited the stand they were not recognised by the new person on the stand and sales were subsequently lost."

A grant will help offset your costs. Your RAB or Arts Council may offer assistance for major trade fairs. The DTI subsidises stands at international trade fairs. Businesses supported by the Prince's Youth Business Trust enjoy substantial assistance. The trust even organise their own showcase within a major trade fair at Birmingham's NEC. Ask at your local business advice centre for information or grants in your area. (See *Yellow Pages* or contact your local TEC in England and Wales or LEC in Scotland.)

Be prepared

It's a good idea to visit a major trade fair before exhibiting. You'll quickly notice those stands which are doing well and those which look rather abandoned. Try to work out why some exhibitors are so successful – observe their manner, display, the stand's position, the work. Knowing how to display work, organise your money and keep your energy levels high will be invaluable.

Apply in good time

Some fairs and markets fill up early and major international trade fairs have long waiting lists. Some operate a selection process and you need to pay special attention to presentation.

Practical preparation might involve attending a pre-fair seminar (offered by the Crafts Council for first-time exhibitors at Chelsea). Knowing how to assemble your display will save time and energy in setting up. Welsh potter, Keith Munroe was ready when he first attended Chelsea: "I had practised building the stand in a friend's garage a couple of days before so I knew where and how each piece was to be displayed on the day."

Good publicity is vital

Take plenty of leaflets, postcards and price lists. For a major trade fair it's important to invite potential buyers. Ken Stradling, Director of the Bristol Guild, recommends makers exhibiting for the first time to send invitations to 20-30 key buyers.

For a trade fair you need examples of your full range of work (known as samples) which can be sold on the last day of the fair. For a fair or market open to the public you'll need to estimate what stock to take. Arrange how to organise your money – you need a float and may want to make special banking arrangements during the fair (though at a fair that is strictly for trade buyers you will just be receiving orders and not making direct cash sales). Make a checklist of everything to take.

Trade fairs

Exhibiting at a trade fair represents a major investment of time and money. Some trade buyers expect to see you there two or three times before they commit themselves to orders. They want reassurance that you are reliable and produce work to a consistent quality.

Victoria Blight, **stained glass artist: how not to arrange your stand.** Photo: the artist

"This was my first trade fair and now I'm more experienced I can see the display just doesn't work. Don't forget trade buyers may be looking at over 300 stands. Yours has to be colourful and eye-catching to get their attention. Try to make sure you aren't at the back of the hall, otherwise buyers will be tired by the time they reach you. If you have a small item that you want to be noticed, display a lot of them together for impact. When I do trade fairs now, I always watch buyers' eyes very closely to observe how they view my stand and rearrange it if necessary. At Top Drawer I found their eyes were drawn to the centre of the stand so I placed the most commercially appealing work there."

How to display

A good display will draw in the customers. When you set up your stand, look at it from a customer's viewpoint. It's a good idea to place a major piece, perhaps something quirky or colourful, as a talking point in a highly visible spot.

Work designed for the domestic environment can be enhanced by creating a classy interior with lighting, mirrors, fabric and flowers.

If work can be worn, wear masses of it. You are part of your display so consider your clothes and presentation carefully. Unless very precious or fragile, work should be accessible and placed so that customers are encouraged to handle it. Place a 'cheap and cheerful' line of brooches or greetings cards at the front.

Some fairs are purely for trade buyers and you should display trade prices. Others are open to the public as well so you need to display

Jane Adam, *Paisley,* mono printed and dyed anodised alumium, 1992. **Photo:** the artist

Jane is a successful jeweller, selling her richly patterned anodised aluminium pieces through trade fairs. She does up to six shows a year and has developed around 100 outlets, mainly in the UK and USA. "It amazes me at a trade show how much you are having to sell yourself. Buyers really need to trust you personally before they'll buy from you. Very often I'll talk to them two or three times before they give me an order. If someone asks me 'What sells?', I don't tell them what I've got most of. I tell them what sells. If it's very inconvenient for me, that's too bad. I think you just need to be honest."

retail prices (equivalent to the selling price in a shop). Trade buyers generally identify themselves quickly but every customer is important. You need to cultivate an alert, professional sales manner which encourages customers without undue pressure.

Success can be gauged both by volume of sales and how popular your stand is. A busy stand draws in other customers and tells people your work is saleable and attractive. They may place orders later. At Art in Action some of the Blue Cat Toy Company's trade buyers visited the stand. Partner Arthur Findlater said: "I was delighted they saw us there. It was a really good advertisement for them to see us selling so well."

A friendly open manner encourages people to look. Engage browsers in conversation and others will stop too. People are nervous of empty space and won't stop if you look bored or preoccupied so don't read or eat on the stand. It's generally recommended to stand and circulate but that's hard on the back and feet for a long show. Experienced exhibitor and buyer Claire Johnson recommends a high stool: "It's comfortable and puts you on the customer's eye level. When you get up from a low chair people feel uneasy at the power shift. They feel slightly guilty because they've disturbed you."

Sales technique

Ask open-ended questions (that cannot be answered 'Yes' or 'No') to establish a rapport with customers. As you learn what they like and sense the price range they are interested in, you can present them with objects that meet their needs. Remember that people buy with emotion and justify with fact. Never, ever, criticise your own work to a customer. It may not be your best piece but it's the one they are interested in. A trade fair isn't a souk so don't rush to haggle over prices – knocking money off may devalue the object in the buyer's eyes.

Trade fair stands are small and you're very close to the customer. At times it's advisable to walk away a few paces, remaining available and attentive. Encouraging people to handle work to promote sales is counter-productive if you make them nervous by watching like a hawk. Pushing too hard for a sale may put customers off. Give them a bit of space and return the moment you spot any buying signals. Gift-wrapping, labelling and placing in a bag are all part of the performance of selling. Customers enjoy the attention, it makes the object feel more precious and others stop to watch the show.

A valuable benefit of a trade fair is the list of customers you come away with. Keep it with great care since the first-time purchaser is likely to buy your work again. Jonathan Andersson keeps a book for each fair, stapling in business cards and brief notes on all who show interest.

A secure approach

Be security-conscious. Shop-lifters are more of a problem at open markets than trade fairs. Most exhibitors use money belts or 'bum-bags'. Be as vigilant with cheques and credit card vouchers as with actual cash. Bank your takings regularly, either in a night safe, or first thing in the morning. Don't count your money in public view.

Many jewellers are unwilling to leave work in the show's safe overnight and prefer to take it home. This may invite criminal attention (eg mugging) so if necessary, organise an escort or taxi to take you and your work home.

Markets

A market doesn't generally have the professional promotion of a trade fair, but it costs less to exhibit and people know about regular markets so they can be a reliable source of income.

Talk to other exhibitors. Take any seasonal factors into account. Christmas, the weather, numbers of tourists all affect levels of sales. With a regular pitch you have to accept such fluctuations.

Try to assess whether a market is genuinely a good selling opportunity. One maker started off doing the larger regional craft markets but gave it up when he realised he sold little and "felt like an unpaid entertainer". Visiting craft markets is a passive form of entertainment for many visitors and selling can be hard work.

As with trade fairs, make your display and sales manner attractive. Teresa Rodrigues finds customers quickly respond to simple display techniques. "I make paper masks. I always put a small spotlight at the front of my stall shining directly on the most popular mask. It's invariably the one that sells first." If the market coincides with a local festival your display might reflect the theme.

Pay attention to price levels. A visitor buying a present or holiday memento will have a definite (often low) price in mind. Only exhibit there if you can sell work at this level and remember your overheads will be less than for a trade fair. On a market stall you might want to concentrate on selling more lower-priced goods, saving the expensive one-offs for galleries and up-market shops.

Practicalities include being prepared for conditions at an outdoor market (layers of warm clothing, wellington boots or sunscreen depending on the weather). Some markets such as Covent Garden Apple Market offer storage arrangements for exhibitors. At an occasional market, you have to pack up at the end of each day and take work home.

Make sure you comply with market regulations displaying a licence where required.

New initiatives

In line with the ACGB report, *Selling the Contemporary Visual Arts*, which found that "the least pretentious, precious, traditional the buying opportunity, the more successful it is", new selling initiatives include non-traditional approaches to fairs and markets.

Three artists collaborated in organising the first Battersea Contemporary Art Fair in 1993. The event provided a commission-free direct selling opportunity for 132 professional artists. Unlike the major art fairs, galleries were excluded. Stands cost just £45 – £95 for the two-day fair and promotion included a catalogue, well-planned press campaign and RAC signposting. Co-organiser Keith Gretton said the response from interested exhibitors was "overwhelming – we could have filled the hall twice over".

Art markets with framed work immediately available are attractive to buyers. Why should a purchaser, spending hundreds of pounds on a painting, have to wait several weeks and comply with rigid gallery conditions before being allowed to collect it? The Contemporary Art Society's annual Art Market, exhibiting work by invited artists, takes work off the wall, wraps it and hands it to the purchaser – just like any regular shop. New stock goes up to replace it, encouraging buyers to visit again.

This cash-and-carry formula has been adopted with success by smaller 'Art Supermarkets'. Many experienced promoters feel this is the way forward for artist-led initiatives, marketing work in accessible, non-gallery environments and encouraging the spontaneous purchaser. During the Manchester Festival, Hope London-Morris organised a two day Art Supermarket, selling work from an empty shop unit. In Madrid, a gallery ran a month-long 'Supermercado de Arte', featuring 30 artists with prices from £40 – £100.

Selling through fairs and markets

ADVANTAGES
- Opportunity to meet customers in person, get feedback and assess competition.
- Large numbers of buyers (UK and overseas) visit trade fairs.
- Your own shopfront to display work and make sales.
- Markets can be source of regular income.
- Gain a valuable mailing list of buyers for future promotions.

DISADVANTAGES
- Trade fair stands are expensive.
- Artists and makers not always confident about selling their work.
- Markets can be unpredictable with sales reduced by factors out of your control.
- Difficult to assess potential success of new ventures.
- Can be disheartening when you don't cover your costs.

7 • Selling from house or studio

A regular or occasional event?

The initial decision to sell direct from the workshop is usually made for you. At some stage most artists and makers will be approached direct by a buyer. Encouraging the public to visit your workplace on a regular basis needs much more consideration.

If you already sell through shops it's advisable to use retail prices when selling direct, perhaps with a small discount. You'll earn more from each sale to compensate for time spent selling and promoting the work and you won't undercut the shops and galleries carrying your work. Selling from house or studio can be an opportunity to sell oddments such as 'seconds' and older work.

Regular hours

If you live in a rural area, attractive to tourists, selling direct from the workshop can be necessary for financial survival. You might decide to open during the summer and over Bank Holiday weekends when there are visitors. In cities and smaller towns, it may be better to open every weekend, particularly if you are near a weekend market.

Once you have decided to open to the public you have to organise your space differently. Creating a separate shop or selling area attached to the studio is a practical solution and may become a legal requirement if you attract a lot of visitors. Painter James Hawkins' studio/gallery near Ullapool in Scotland has become an established stop on the tourist trail. Established over ten years ago, it now turns over £50,000 per year with 75% of sales to visitors.

Caroline Bousfield Gregory is a potter working in Hackney. She advertises her studio/shop Workshop in *Crafts* magazine and enjoys the contact with visitors but, as she is out of the main commercial area, doesn't attract so many people as to disrupt the working day. "I very much enjoy selling direct to the public. People are so interesting. Groups of children from local schools come to visit . There are so few places where you can watch things being made – the shoe-menders is probably the only other place round here! Apparently Hackney has as many artists working in the borough as Paris and I find it sad that so few of them are visible from the street."

Operating a permanent gallery/shop on your premises means advertising opening hours. 'By appointment only' can be fine during the winter but it tends to discourage visitors and you won't attract passing

John Leach, **the Pottery Shop at Muchelney Pottery in Somerset carries the classic range of hand-thrown kitchen pots together with 'one-off' signed original pots. John is one of the few craftspeople who uses a marketing specialist to write copy and produce his publicity leaflets and posters. These invite visitors to the Pottery and are distributed through Tourist Information Centres, local hotels and bed-and-breakfasts. The shop is open all year round and the workshop by appointment only.**

trade that way. Make sure you have reliable family or friends to cover the advertised opening hours when required.

Occasional sales

For many artists and makers, a constant flow of visitors to the workshop would be too disruptive and make it impossible for them to work. They therefore sell direct on an occasional, planned basis.

A pre-Christmas or summer sale is an excellent opportunity to invite previous purchasers, friends and family. When several artists and makers do a combined sale, an interesting range of work is shown and you have the advantage of sharing customers and organisation. You might decide to sell from your own studio (or home). But if more of your buyers live elsewhere, don't feel restricted to your own area. It's always possible to organise it at a friend's home.

Sue Dunkley, *Northern Sky*, charcoal drawing, 22"x30".

Sue has organised three successful studio sales of her work between 1986 and 1992. "I was getting a bit frustrated with gallery shows and felt I was more motivated than gallery staff to sell my work. So I organised a three-day studio sale over a weekend, got a friend to help me hang the work, labelled it clearly, printed lots of price lists, tidied up the house and bought plenty of wine. I circulated a large mailing list and did some local advertising for the first event. Lots of people came and brought their friends and I sold plenty of work. I invited my window cleaner and he brought two friends who spent £1000. Now people often find me by word of mouth. I think all artists should experience selling this way. Get organised and make sure you have someone there to help you."

A Christmas sale of painted clothes and wall panels by Carole Waller, jewellery by Leonardo Pieroni and drawings by Michael Westley was held in the London house of a friend of Carole's. The artists pooled mailing lists, sent out flyers and invited people to RSVP. Michael Westley was particularly pleased with the event, selling 60% of his framed charcoal and wash drawings. They are planning a second joint sale in another friend's house. Use of the house plus drinks for invited guests were offered in return for a modest percentage on sales.

Elsewhere a special sale might be organised around an event such as a kiln firing. John Leach advertised in *The Independent on Sunday*, *Ceramic Review* and *Crafts* attracting visitors to the three-day loading, firing and grand opening of the kiln at Muchelney Pottery and sold work over the weekend event.

Open studios

Open studios are a popular way for artists to show their work. They can be a good way of selling as well. How you organise and publicise the event depends on what type of studio you work in.

The best known open studios are where a number of artists, working in the same building or artists' studio group, collaborate in a large, highly visible event. Weekend opens at WASPS studios in

Edinburgh and Balls Pond Studios in London are among those which have attracted interest. Other events cover a larger geographical area and encourage artists' groups and individuals to participate. Studios across the East End of London open for an extended period around the Whitechapel Open Exhibition. Oxford Artweek has publicised artists' and craftspeople's studios around the county including maps to help find the most isolated workshops.

There are advantages to working in a group: costs, organisation, contacts, ideas and skills can be shared. It's best if the group have worked together before. Divide up the work involved in organising the event right at the beginning, as with a group exhibition.

See 8 • Exhibitions

Plan well in advance so you have time to apply for grants or fund-raise to help with publicity. Sort out your priorities among the group so that publicity is targeted appropriately. For an artists' studio group, the most important aspect is often community access, a rare opportunity to open the studio doors to the public, let people know what actually goes on there and meet the artists. Another priority might be gaining critical acclaim in which case you may decide to create a gallery-type environment and invite critics, gallery owners, other artists and collectors.

But if selling is high on the list of priorities, make this clear in the organisation, display and promotion of the event. Try to create an atmosphere in your studio which is conducive to selling – clearly displayed prices, uncluttered presentation, good lighting, framed work, CVs and cards with your name and phone number that people can take away with them. Sort out in advance how you will deal with sales. Sue Dunkley gets standing order forms from the bank so that people can pay by instalments. Have packing materials to hand and let people take work away immediately. There's nothing more guaranteed to create a selling buzz than seeing people leaving with canvasses they have just bought.

Whether you are intent on selling or showing through an open studio, make the studio safe and clear away any machinery or chemicals. Clean the place up but not beyond recognition. It is a working environment and non-artists are fascinated by the equipment, materials, pinboard, sketchbooks and anything that gives a clue to the artist's inspiration and working methods. Talking in a straightforward way about what you look at, what inspires you and how you make work can be the starting point for encouraging a new buyer, wary of contemporary art and lacking confidence in their taste and judgement.

Practical & legal considerations

See 15 • Selling & the law
Anyone inviting the public into their home or workshop to buy work encounters a set of practical and legal questions.

Insurance

Are you covered for public liability? A maker's workshop may contain industrial machinery, sharp tools and dangerous chemicals and you could be liable if someone had an accident there. Jane Adam says: "I've got public liability on my insurance, it's the most expensive section but my insurance broker made me have it. I'm glad it's there. Anybody coming into the studio, whether a student, tax inspector or customer is protected." Public liability is the law for premises open to the public and is increasingly common on home insurance policies.

Alternatively, you don't need public liability insurance if people come 'by invitation only'. You have to word all publicity carefully with this phrase and 'invitations are available from ... .' An advertisement or press release can state 'this acts as an invitation, please bring it with you'. You need to have someone on the door, signing in all visitors and issuing 'invitations' to anyone who turns up without one. But this wouldn't prevent someone from suing you if they had an accident.

Permission & regulations

For occasional or small-scale sales you may need permission from your landlord. To trade on a more regular basis, you may have to consult your mortgage-holder or landlord, and the planning authority (district or borough council).

Planning permission for selling work from the home or studio is a grey area and is interpreted differently across the country. Basically, you do not need to apply for a change of use unless: the business affects the nature of the house, eg where you do building work to create a shop or gallery; you are externally attracting customers; you employ people within the home. Current advice seems to be that, unless the numbers of visitors and deliveries regularly takes the level of trade to a point where it is seen to cause a disturbance to the neighbourhood, you don't need to worry about planning consent. Contact your local planning department for advice.

Once you open a shop or gallery on your premises you have to pay business rates and may need to observe relevant fire and safety standards. Again contact the local authority for advice. With business rates you should contact the planning department and then the rates department (who will then contact the Inland Revenue for a valuation). For fire and safety ask who the relevant officers are. All these officials

Decorative & Applied Arts in Dorset **is a well-designed free leaflet featuring around 30 Dorset-based makers. Leaflet design by Foothold. Six thematic craft trails are described with good quality photographs, descriptions and opening hours to encourage visitors to buy or commission work direct from the maker. The leaflet was jointly commissioned by South West Arts, Southern Arts and Dorset County Council. A sister leaflet for Hampshire, The Treasure Trove, was commissioned by Hampshire County Council and Southern Arts. It promotes the county's "decorative arts treasures" and publicises the work of contemporary artists and craftspeople making to commission. Rosalind Marchant researched the two leaflets which are designed to complement each other and to appeal to both residents and visitors.**

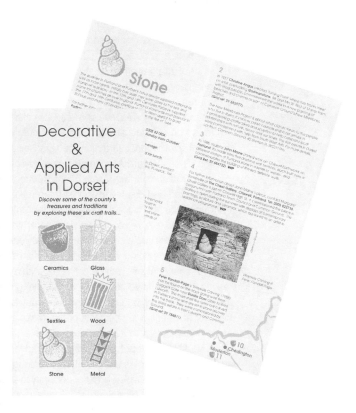

work to statutory regulations, but they are not there to put you out of business. Don't be afraid of asking their advice or trying to negotiate with them.

Security

This is an important consideration for artists and makers, particularly women, working alone. When inviting people to a sale of work in your home, consider it as a private party. Have a selected guest list and ask people to RSVP. If you anticipate large numbers for a studio or home sale, set up a sales counter near the exit. Make sure work sells and doesn't walk out. Getting someone to help you is a very good idea. This may mean paying someone, but if you are doing a one-off maybe you could get a friend to help, or another artist and then you could do the same for them.

Promotion

See 3 • Making marketing work for you

Opening a shop-gallery on the premises, you need to devote considerable time and resources to marketing. As with any shop, people need to know you are there and be persuaded to visit.

If you are well off the beaten track, target publicity carefully. Make sure people find you through free listings or guidebooks used by visitors to the area, eg *Visiting Craft Workshops in the English Countryside* published by the Rural Development Commission. The Tourist Board will advise on signage and through the Council can organise placing traditional brown tourist attraction road signs at a charge of around £50 per sign. The RAC and AA can also give advice.

A craft shop or art gallery might produce a leaflet and A4 poster for distribution and display in Tourist Information Centres, local hotels and guest houses, bookshops and restaurants. Look at a range of leaflets and make sure your design is eyecatching and will appeal to the sort of customers you want to attract. Get advice on print run length and check distribution points regularly to replenish stocks.

A seasonal sale can be promoted with a stylish invitation which needn't be expensive to produce. Simple graphic design is most effective. For open studios, where you want to attract more people, consider advertising in specialist press. Make use of free listings and target local media with a lively press release.

With a group open studio, one of the advantages is that everyone invites their friends plus people who have bought work or visited their exhibitions in the past. It's a great opportunity to expand the audience for your work and well worth asking visitors to leave their names and addresses for further information.

Selling from house or studio

ADVANTAGES
- Greater profit on sales as you keep commission.
- Control display and presentation of the work.
- Meet customers, get feedback and get purchasers' names for future promotions.
- No time wasted on packing and transporting work to other outlets.

DISADVANTAGES
- Constant interruptions disrupt your concentration and work pattern.
- Expensive alterations may be necessary to meet planning regulations.
- Creating a selling area in home or studio restricts workspace.
- Direct contact with customers difficult for the shy or unassertive.

8 • Exhibitions

Selling may be among your reasons for taking part in an exhibition but is rarely top of the list. A successful exhibition can be judged in terms of critical acclaim, visitor numbers, the chance to develop and show a new body of work as well as sales figures. But exhibiting your work does involve additional work and expense. Make sure you maximise the selling and promotional opportunity of an exhibition.

Taking part in an exhibition

There are a wide range of exhibition opportunities, many listed in *Artists Newsletter:* open submission, themed, invitation only, for members, open to local artists as well as individual shows. Submissions may be by slide or actual work, often with a fee and the artist, whether accepted or rejected, usually pays for transport and framing.

The organisers normally take a commission on sales, usually less than a shop and in some cases as low as 10%. Some artists sell exclusively through exhibitions. Basket-maker Polly Pollock makes colourful work, using card, tape and other recycled materials. Mostly she sells and gets commissions through exhibitions. "The mark-up in shops just makes my work too pricy. People can see the materials aren't expensive and won't pay those prices."

Competition for widely-advertised open exhibitions is fierce. Choose work with care and present it professionally. Selectors themselves admit that large open exhibitions are something of a lottery. They may only have a few seconds to view work so don't take a rejection to heart.

Artists and makers are generally advised to pursue every exhibition opportunity at the early stages of their career. Large mixed shows and themed open exhibitions are rarely prime selling opportunities. However, they are an excellent means of self-promotion. List every exhibition on your CV and add the catalogue or leaflet to your marketing

Louise Barber, *Painted Structure,* work created for the Ernst and Young building's atrium, Bristol.
Photo: the artist

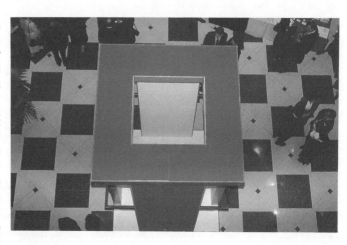

In 1991 Ernst and Young approached Artspace Studios in Bristol to organise a selling exhibition for the accountancy firm's Christmas party. They wanted to create a colourful and adventurous show and made a daring selection of work which was displayed in the company's offices. Ernst and Young covered basic transport and display costs. A successful show resulted with sales and the opportunity to reach a new buying public. Artspace artists were invited back in 1992. With experience of what people were interested in buying, they provided a different show, exhibiting a greater selection of smaller work, and sales increased.

folder. As your experience, and CV, grows, become more selective and enter only those where exhibition prizes, professional marketing, a prestigious venue or selection panel offer added incentives.

With an individual exhibition, there may be room for negotiation over sales commission. A photographer, working in partnership with her sister as her business manager, built up a substantial mailing list of previous purchasers. They have negotiated a lower percentage commission on private views in exchange for organising and publicising them.

Organise your own

Whether as an individual or with others, this can be an extremely rewarding experience. *Organising Your Exhibition* by Debbie Duffin is essential reading.

Hired space

Exhibition space can be hired. Costs vary and must be included in your overheads. Gallery space with white walls, lighting track and a mailing list offers certain advantages. But the space must suit your work and the existing gallery clientele be those you want to attract.

Other public spaces are cheap to hire and encourage more imaginative promotion. A group of 13 artists, calling themselves the CIA (Contemporary International Artists) hired a church hall in South Kensington for two weeks. Vanilla Beer took part: "We all put up our work and put out trestle tables and tried to harass people in. Everybody's

BANK group, *Chlorine*, **installation by** John Russell, Simon Bedwell **and** Dino Demosthenous **in disused swimming pool, Soho, 1992.**

BANK is a group of young artists living and working in London who create exhibitions in unusual and difficult spaces. They have worked in a disused bank in Lewisham, a swimming pool in Soho and a freight warehouse near Kings Cross. They view the show as the product, and imaginative approaches to sponsors have succeeded in raising funds to cover costs. Pro-moting wider access to the visual arts is the prime objective although occasion-ally individual sales of work do result. For one show, 'Quick Print' photo company sponsored the catalogue by producing thousands of photographs of works at very low cost. These were spiral bound into instant, limited edition catalogues.

friends came and, being in South Ken, most people spent a lot so it was quite a good moneyspinner. The big problem was staffing. You have 13 people, ten of whom think they don't have to do anything. Basically one of us took it on board."

Create your own exhibition space

Some of the most exciting exhibition initiatives in recent years have come from artists creating their own space in unexpected places. The recession has left unlet units in shopping malls which artists' groups in Exeter, Southampton, Bristol and Milton Keynes have taken over. Unused offices and industrial units have become temporary galleries.

Group initiatives

Many successful selling exhibitions are organised by groups. Member organisations can have an advantage in applying for grants or exhibitions in recognised venues. Debbie Duffin stresses the importance of shared organisation with group events: "whenever you are working with others, it is important from the outset that it is clear who is responsible for what". A simple checklist of tasks to allocate to different people would be:

- finding and preparing exhibition space
- fund-raising
- accounts
- administration
- transport
- publicity material
- publicity distribution
- staffing rota
- organising private view.

Publicity and promotion

See 3 • Making marketing work for you

A successfully promoted exhibition will be talked about before being seen. It's essential to create a publicity budget, however small. When deciding what form your publicity should take, consider what messages you want to convey. What 'benefits' in marketing terms does the exhibition offer your target audience? How can you best communicate these? Exhibition publicity material might include some of the following:

- poster: A4-A1 size, monochrome to full colour
- catalogue
- price list
- private view invitations
- postcards
- leaflet or flyer
- press releases.

Publicity material doesn't have to be expensive to be effective. One of the key factors is distribution. With a selling exhibition, carefully target publicity to groups and individuals you want to attract. A select mailing list of named individuals working in specific professions or living in a particular area will be more useful than large and indiscriminate mailings.

When a gallery is organising your exhibition, don't rely on them exclusively for the publicity. It's worth investing your own time in targeting private view invitations. Sue Dunkley had a gallery exhibition in 1993 showing paintings from time spent in Ireland. With experience of selling

Angela Edmonds, *On Site III* (detail), charcoal on paper, 1992, 4'x3'. **Photo:** the artist

Angela became interested in a building site under develop-ment in her home town of Watford in 1989. Over the next three years she produced a series of drawings showing the growth of the Harlequin Centre. Although the work was entirely self-initiated, the developers Capital & Counties Plc became involved and arranged site visits for her. They recognised this was a unique record of the changing aspects of the site and eventually purchased a large body of work. In 1992 they put on an exhibition in the Centre and bought further drawings. Although they had not originally included an artist in their plans they became genuinely interested after seeing some of the work and realising its potential.

her own work, she decided to target London solicitors and other professionals with Irish names and spent hours going through Yellow Pages to compile a mailing list.

When organising your own exhibition, a poster and leaflet should put your message across clearly. A useful principle for such publicity is AIDA: in other words it should Attract, Inform, create Desire, encourage Action.

A simply-produced small flyer printed in tones of red was distributed by Cromwell & Ward Gallery in London to local offices and businesses in the Covent Garden area, publicising their 'Great Art Sale'. Basic but effective graphic design made the key marketing messages stand out: "All original work ... Over 40 top Artists ... Nothing over £500 – Some as low as £50." The leaflet stated: "We believe in promoting top contemporary art at affordable prices from established artists and talented newcomers" and invited you to "bring this leaflet for a free glass of wine". If you are organising a selling exhibition, be direct in the messages your publicity conveys and don't be afraid of enticing the public in with free offers – of wine, postcards, posters, etc.

Take advantage of free listings in local event magazines or newspapers. Media coverage does increase attendance – send press releases to local papers, radio and TV. Follow up with a phone call to the editor. Ring up first and ask who to send information to and what they would like.

Make sure the prices are clear. There is nothing designed to discourage sales more than having to pay to enter a selling exhibition and then buy the price list. All invigilators need to be briefed about selling and to understand how to deal confidently with a sales enquiry. Prepare a folder with artists' CVs and postcards or business cards so that the invigilator can provide additional information and offer the means of contacting an artist direct. Take them round the show and talk to them about the work before the exhibition opens.

The private view is generally where most work is sold. A well-organised private view is an attractive opportunity for both artist and gallery to welcome existing and potential purchasers. Use it to its best advantage. Don't allow it to become a private party for friends that gives other people a feeling of being excluded. With a group exhibition, sort out how you will deal with sales. A practical solution is for one person to take on the role of sales manager for the private view. You can extend the private view situation by offering special talks or tours to groups you think are potential buyers – or offering the gallery space to host other events.

Do encourage exhibition visitors to sign in with full addresses so you can invite them to future events. The visitor's book is often seen as unnecessary gallery bureaucracy but with attention and friendly persuasion, you can gain valuable additions to your mailing list.

Selling through exhibitions

ADVANTAGES
• Exhibitions can help you achieve your goals as an artist.
• Commercial gallery exhibitions have trained staff eager to sell.
• Reviews and catalogue entries all help market your work elsewhere.
• Exhibition sales encourage viewers to consider your work more seriously.
• Organising your own exhibition means you control presentation and retain profits.

DISADVANTAGES
• Much effort for a place in open exhibitions but few sales.
• In open shows your work may be badly hung and poorly lit.
• Organising your own exhibition is expensive, you could make a loss.
• Organising a group exhibition is time-consuming, you may fall out with friends over it.

9 • Agents: the great myth?

Artists Newsletter Information Service and RABs regularly receive requests from artists and makers to 'recommend a good agent'. Unfortunately, the idea that there are scores of Hollywood-style agents desperate to sign up talented artists is largely a myth. Economics are against it. Agents are business people, good at selling, who act as middlemen, or women, between producer and buyer.

They earn a percentage on every sale and must sell either in great quantity or at very high prices to make a living. The amount of contemporary art and craft work sold is just not sufficient to support a tier of agents. In a recession, the financial viability of the agent's position is particularly vulnerable. Most artists and makers therefore act as their own agents and, through necessity, develop the selling skills and contacts required.

As you gain experience and find the right shops, galleries and dealers to sell your work, these outlets become your agents, developing and sustaining a profitable relationship with buyers of your work.

Some artists dislike the business of selling so much that they develop an informal arrangement with a friend or fellow artist to act as their agent. Printmaker Sheila Clarkson works in this way: "I find it very difficult to go into a gallery. My work is so personal, like a diary. Opening up my portfolio, it's like taking all my clothes off in the middle of the shop and saying 'What do you think of this?' You make yourself very vulnerable, whereas by doing it through an agent, they go into the gallery and talk in the right language in a way I can't because I refuse to do it."

Agents offer two key advantages: quantity, or range of work, and contacts. Agents can be more successful in meeting buyers since they can show a lot of work by different artists. Buyers are interested in choice and diversity. A good agent also has more contacts than an individual maker or artist can usually manage. Selling is their business and they put substantial efforts into developing a relationship with potential buyers.

There are certain areas of selling contemporary visual art where agents exist and may offer advantages over the individual approach.

Autograph, **newsletter cover photograph by Franklyn Rodgers. Autograph is the Association of Black Photographers, established as a forum for photographers in Britain of African, Caribbean and South Asian origin. Around 300 members' slides are kept on register and Autograph acts as a broker across a number of areas. They publish catalogues and books and a Directory of Black Photographers. They also act as an agent obtaining commissions and selling library pictures by members.**

Before committing yourself to representation by an agent, research their track record. Ask which other artists or makers they represent and contact these for an informal reference. If the agent is unwilling to say who else they sell, there may be a good reason but you need to find another way of checking them out. Assess the amount of work they carry – too much and your work won't stand out, too little and they may not be financially viable or be too inexperienced to represent you well. What about the quality of work carried – does it enhance yours, or make it look cheap?

You should always put all arrangements with an agent in writing. Both parties should sign and date this document which is the contract between them. A useful checklist of points to include is:

- Financial arrangement – commission percentage, date of payment. Can the agent demand their commission before the buyer has paid up?
- Is the agent responsible for care of work in their possession? Eg are they insuring it, or are they liable for damage or theft?
- Does the agent have the exclusive right to represent you? Many shops or galleries, even when dealing through an agent, want to have direct contact with the artist.
- Who is responsible for promotional material?
- How long the agreement lasts.
- What area it covers (eg UK only).
- What circumstances will allow you and/or the agent to terminate the agreement (eg lack of sales) and what notice is required.
- Return of work, slides, etc.
- Selling price.

Remember, anyone can set themselves up as an agent and there is no guarantee of sales. A bad agent can not only neglect to sell your work but actively damage your reputation. A textile artist was obliged to sever her agreement with an agent whose unpleasant manner was alienating all her best outlets. Only when she resumed direct contact with the shops did she discover why orders had dropped off.

Gavin Rookledge, *Folder,* black goatskin with beaten steel and cast bronze.

Photo: Hayde Sacerdote

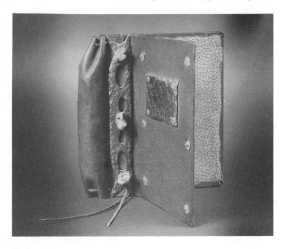

Gavin is a book artist creating handmade bindings using a range of forms and materials. In 1992, trading as Rook's Books, he did his first major selling show at Chelsea Crafts Fair and received substantial orders. "I was approached by a Japanese agent who ordered a range of samples costing £1000. In the next three months, he placed a £1300 order followed by another worth £1000. From the start I insisted on advance payment by banker's transfer which has worked well. I've had to learn everything about shipping and dealing with agents very quickly. He wants exclusive rights and I'm not sure how long to limit it for. My only problem since the business took off is that I've always said 'yes' to orders. Now I'm so busy, I'm having to learn to say 'yes, but not immediately'. I'm exhausted as I've only had two days off in five months but I've just found a skilled assistant which should help."

Artists' agents

Difficult to find and often hard to manage the relationship. As sales through agents incur commission and increase prices, galleries prefer to act on recommendations or direct contact with artists.

The most positive approach seems to be the 'active portfolio' where an agent holds slides or examples of work by 100 or more artists. Ian Way started Artway in South West England in 1990, promoting the work of 120 artists through a portfolio and slide register. He recognises the difficulty of selling original work and has broadened his activities beyond the agent's role. Approaches to councils and museums have been successful in the past although as their budgets are reduced he sees this as a decreasing market.

Craft agents

Few makers of one-off or limited range high quality work sell through agents. And, as with visual artists, galleries and shops are generally not interested in buying from agents. For the smaller outlet, contact with the maker is essential for them to recognise the unique qualities of the work, and helps them sell it.

Craftspeople seeking wide distribution of their work, to high street chains and gift shops may find agents suitable for them. Such makers will usually be producing in quantity and be experienced at selling through trade fairs to a range of buyers before reaching this stage.

Photographers' & illustrators' agents

Useful for promoting your work in the commercial field but not essential for success. Illustrator Carmel Hayes recommends getting experience of seeking work yourself before signing up with an agent. She says most agents only look for advertising and design work which pays best. Even with an agent you still have to find your own editorial and publishing work.

Overseas agents

Overseas department store agents based in the UK and foreign agents may be part of your distribution network for selling work abroad . In this situation, the contacts and local knowledge an agent offers can be essential to marketing your work successfully in another country. But make sure you establish a contract with an overseas agent since it is difficult to negotiate at a distance. The DTI can give advice on making contacts overseas.

Christian Funnel makes sculptural furniture using metal and recycled objects. He experienced problems with a Paris agent who ordered four pieces after seeing his work in a London shop. He shipped the work over but the agent decided they didn't like it and refused to pay. Eventually it was returned, but the artist paid £50 carriage and was throughly disillusioned about this way of selling.

Selling through agents

ADVANTAGES

- Specialist agents useful in some sales environments.
- Agents have more commercial contacts.
- Highly motivated salespeople.
- Leave you more time to make.

DISADVANTAGES

- Usually only interested in you when you already sell well.
- Sales commission cuts your profits.
- May push for large orders of cheaper work.
- You lose contact with customers.
- Agents may not represent you as you want to be seen.

10 • Working to commission

Working to commission can be a rewarding way of selling. Success usually comes with experience. It's important to understand the process, and pitfalls, of working this way.

Whether for a public space or private individual, the making of a commissioned piece involves substantial consultation with the client. Although you have been hired as a professional artist or maker, decisions on form, size, materials or colour may be strongly influenced by the client.

At best, the consultation process is a creative dialogue resulting in a piece that meets the aspirations of both client and artist. At worst, you may end up producing an unsatisfactory piece, compromised by budgetary and other constraints.

Public commissions

Most public commissions require an approach to negotiating, pricing and working that is not within the scope of this book. But some may be looking for an artist to make a specific piece of work that the commissioner simply buys. Any artist seeking to undertake public commissions should seek advice from public art agencies, artists, and other experienced professionals.

There is great scope for artists and makers to create works in a public context and increasing interest from developers, architects and planners. Work in this field demands a complex set of skills. You may have to manage a large budget, understand planning regulations and interpret architects' specifications as well as know how to negotiate a contract.

Particular sensitivity to the context is required from the artist since others will live with your work every day. Anne Toms was commissioned to paint a decorative panel for Southampton General Hospital's children's ward. "You have to be so careful not to paint anything that might disturb or frighten a child ... eyes, dark shadowy shapes, flashes of red could all seem threatening."

Robert Soden, *Cranes Noonday* Canary Wharf, mixed media on paper, 1990, 32"x42".

Through an interest in buildings and factories, artist Robert Soden has developed a wide experience of commissions including works for Customs and Excise, British Gas and the Laird Group. In the late 1980s, as a result of a commission to record the Banker's Trust building at Broadgate, works hung in the company's foyer as part of their art collection attracted the attention of some estate agents. They suggested he look at new developments in Docklands ("If you like cranes – go to Canary Wharf"). Robert did a series of self-initiated paintings there and approached the art buyer for developers Olympia and York. She purchased five paintings for the offices and boardroom and Robert also sold work to an engineer working on the project. He points out that commissions have given him access to extraordinary sites, such as a rooftop above the Broadgate development. And, unlike portrait painters, the architectural artist has tremendous freedom since "buildings can't answer back".

Many such commissions are managed by public art and private design agencies. Working within a large budget, often determined as a percentage of the total development costs, there are real advantages to working with specialists who can negotiate, promote, research and argue on your behalf. They act as the go-between in what is often a new relationship between artist and developer.

Private commissions

Private commissioning is more like a 'sale' than a public commission is. The difference between the private commission and a straightforward sale is that the buyer is taking the initiative – and maybe even describing what they want. A private commission can be as simple as a jeweller making a special piece for a customer who wants a particular combination of form, pattern and colour.

The most exciting private commissions are where the artist or maker creates something unique as a special gift, perhaps a christening or retirement present or an awards trophy. The commissioning process can provide fresh inspiration. Incorporating personal detail related to the recipient's life and interests enhances the distinctiveness of a piece.

An exhibition by the Society of Designer Craftsmen, The Commissioning Dialogue, featured objects as diverse as a sundial by sculptor Quin Hollick, a baby's bowl by silversmith Peter Mason and a laundry basket made of painted woven cardboard by Polly Pollock.

The Federation of British Artists promotes members' work, offering a free advice service for clients. Having discussed the commission informally, a shortlist of studios is provided to select an artist. Individual and family portraits, animals and houses are popular commissions.

Commissioned paintings, especially portraits, can be a difficult area for artists. They often feel constrained to create the image the commissioner requires. Lucy Willis now only does private commissions for friends or where she finds it particularly interesting: "In the past I have regretted taking on commissions. You're basically fulfilling someone else's idea." Vanilla Beer used to make a living doing portraits but "I found it just ghastly. I enjoyed the work but got nothing from it. I felt very damaged as an artist by it. Now I still do portraits but only when I want to and if I don't have to do what people expect of me."

Christian Funnell developed work doing temporary installations for trade fairs. With a partner he created dramatic displays for fashion and sports equipment companies. Their first commission was a surfwear company exhibiting at the Paris Boat Show. "We made an outrageous display with paintings and tons of old tyres. It was absolutely shocking alongside the perfect fibreglass sailing boats and surfboards. The owner was totally panic-stricken when he saw what we had done. He tried to disown his stand but soon realised that everyone liked it. He took a hell of a risk but it worked out OK in the end." After four other fashion shows, Christian now finds this area of commissioned work has dried up during the recession.

Contracts & copyright

Agreeing a price and getting paid for commissioned work is not always straightforward. Artists are advised to protect themselves by agreeing all details of the commissioned piece (materials, cost, size, delivery date, payment schedule, etc) in a written contract.

Take care with pricing: get quotes for materials and calculate your time generously. An initial deposit of 50% is normal for private commissions. Public commissions have a more complex schedule with defined payment stages. Some people are indecisive and others really enjoy contact with an artist or maker, so allow time for meetings and the social aspects of commissioning when pricing a work.

Don't forget the contract is there to protect both sides. A privately commissioned gift not ready in time for the retirement presentation or anniversary party may be deemed by the client to have lost its value. Keep the client informed about any delays in completion.

Unless agreed otherwise, copyright of a commissioned work remains with the artist. The artist has the exclusive right to reproduce it, as prints or cards for example.

Promotion

Many public and private commissions come through agencies who hold examples of artists' work, often on slide indexes, and publicise their service to potential commissioners. The agency may be actively involved in the commissioning process and charge a fee to clients for their services. A 1990 survey suggested that some 39% of artists are on a slide index.

Good quality slides are essential. Many indexes are slow to check and update artists' details. It's up to you to inform the organisation of any changes and make sure you update your slides periodically.

The future for slide indexes, which quickly become unwieldy to manage, is computerisation. This means that images are scanned and stored on computer to be linked with textual databases. Information can be accessed on a computer screen, stored on compact disk (CD) or video disk. These systems are known as multi-media. The Crafts Council is developing a national picture library of crafts to be available in the future on computer throughout the country. It will hold 35,000 images from their slide library and other images from *Crafts* magazine. AXIS: Visual Arts Information Service is developing a multi-media register of work by artists, craftspeople and photographers in England, Scotland and Wales. Sight Specific holds a multimedia index of 250 personally selected makers, which can be transferred to photo CD or video, for use by architects and developers in commissioning building-based work.

Invest in good quality photographs of finished commissions and they may be used for leaflets, annual reports and magazines. Getting your work in print helps promote yourself and get more commissions.

Selling through commissioned work

ADVANTAGES
• Opportunity to create distinctive, often larger, pieces.
• Excellent promotion opportunity.
• One commission often leads to another.

DISADVANTAGES
• Consultation process can compromise final piece.
• Budget and payment problems if public art fund-raising unsuccessful.
• Pricing difficult as many unknown factors.

11 • More selling opportunities

Magazines & directories

An attractive selling option which has broken new ground is *Art for Sale* distributed by *The Guardian*. The first two issues in 1992 featured around 400 works, mostly paintings, by contemporary artists. Presenting itself as 'the catalogue of British art today', the magazine offered works priced £250 – £7000. Work was displayed in a London gallery but much sold straight off the page, the buyer seeing only a small colour reproduction and minimal biographical details for the artist.

Art for Sale plans to publish on a regular basis, is developing its own New Art Club and looks set to take the selling of contemporary art out of the gallery setting and into an accessible format which buyers respond to. There's strong competition among artists for inclusion: for the second issue, 200 artists were selected from 10,000 slides received.

Artists and designer-makers successful at selling and exhibiting their work are often invited to advertise in promotional directories. These buyers' guides or catalogues are viewed with some suspicion by experienced artists. Don't be persuaded to part with money until you are convinced you are buying into a good quality, well-distributed publication. Ask how work has been selected, what advertising will be carried and how the catalogue will be distributed, and contact artists already listed for feedback.

Mail order

Selling through mail order is most suitable for people producing work in quantity, eg craftspeople making 'repeats' and printmakers. Before deciding to do mail order, make sure your work can be easily packaged. Work out your prices to include packing (time and materials), postage or courier delivery and insurance where necessary.

Advertising in interior design magazines can cost several hundred pounds. It may be worthwhile for saleable gift objects, especially before Christmas, but assess advertising costs carefully since the same amount of time and money may produce better results elsewhere.

Vanilla Beer, *Pauses that are as good as death*.
Photo: Bernard Heslin

Vanilla has a healthy scepticism about the art market and gallery system for selling work: "I think selling your real work is bloody difficult and if it's selling easily the chances are you're doing something wrong." Some of her work is ephemeral and destined to be unsaleable, using materials such as ice, shadow, talc, wax and oil. With a group of artists in South London she is currently negotiating to take on a huge space rent-free from the council in Greenwich. There would be studios, a gallery and community workshops. They plan to hold monthly exhibitions, each ending with an auction to sell off all the work. Vanilla says: "The auctions would be a regular event and a lively occasion. Work would be cheap, maybe just a few pounds. We've even got an auctioneer on our Committee."

Mail order sales require efficient organisation, eg taking credit card orders by phone and sending catalogues. Goods should normally be delivered within 28 days or an acknowledgement sent confirming the delivery date. Consumer legislation protects purchasers of mail order items. They can claim a refund if goods arrive damaged. Goods can be returned if they are not 'as described' and in most cases, if the purchaser decides they do not want the goods, they can claim a refund if goods are returned undamaged within 7-14 days.

An order for a mail order catalogue is a good selling opportunity. Organisations like Greenpeace, Friends of the Earth and the National Trust produce high quality gift catalogues and regularly commission makers and illustrators to create work for them. Price is critical and your name may not feature in the catalogue but work is usually well photographed and reproduced in full colour. Ceramic makers Reptile made a whale panel for the Greenpeace catalogue. 75 were ordered initially with a smaller follow-up order. Another ceramicist was commissioned to make hand-painted mugs which were so successful that the initial order of 300 led to a further order of 250.

Mail order is a big selling opportunity in the USA with a huge volume of catalogue sales. Frannie has had a number of orders through the UK buying agent for a major US department store. She supplied 3,000 pairs of cufflinks and had to get help making up such a large order. They also ordered silk waistcoats and braces for the catalogue. If you are entering such a potentially large selling market you should be prepared to cope with the scale of production it could generate.

Auctions

A few select artists and makers sell their work through auctions although this way of selling has declined in the 90s. It offers a prestigious sales environment which has been successful, notably for studio pottery.

Others are invited to donate work to auctions in aid of various causes. While this cannot be seen as a real selling opportunity for the artist, it does give the experience of seeing work valued on the open market. It can be disheartening if work is sold at a charity auction for substantially less than its value but few artists could afford to give the actual money to support the campaign. And, who knows, the person who buys your work might want to buy another piece, so make sure they know where to find you.

Collections

Public and corporate art collections rarely feature as selling opportunities for artists and makers. But they do have purchasing budgets and regularly buy work. The difficulty is identifying them and making the right approach. A very few advertise themselves. South East Arts maintains a collection of contemporary art and every year invite artists in the region to submit slides. After studio visits, selected work is bought and made available for loan to public buildings in the region.

Tracking down other collections and defining their purchasing policy is more complicated. Painter and printmaker Yolanda Christian researched a number of institutions but warned in an article in *Artists Newsletter* that individual artists should not send material or applications on spec. She described the perseverance and confidence artists need to establish a rapport with collection curators: "For the unrepresented artist it can be difficult to get past the cold shoulder routine, expensive tracking people down and is, once the euphoria of a success has subsided, in hindsight, not financially viable time-wise but largely a prestige and self-satisfying activity." Nevertheless, she managed to persuade curators in the Midlands to visit her London studio resulting in purchases and exhibitions.

Always feature collection purchases prominently on your CV. And make sure, if your work sells through a gallery that they inform you if work is bought by a public collection. The normal convention of not informing artists who buys work should be overruled in this case.

Mark Lewis, *Straining at the leash,* galvanised steel tube and leather bike seat, 1992.

Photo: the artist

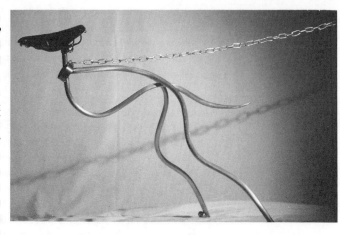

Sculptural furniture designer Mark Lewis won the design section of European Vision, a competition organised through the Prince's Trusts. The local Buckinghamshire paper publicised his success and brought him to the attention of the High Wycombe Chair Museum. They approached him and are currently negotiating buying one of his pieces for their collection.

Competitions

Competitions may not, strictly speaking, be selling opportunities. But they offer excellent marketing potential. There may be prizes of cash, commissions, materials, travel or other goods. The attraction of a good selection panel is sufficient incentive for many artists and often an exhibition of selected work will be organised. After applying for seven years, painter Lucy Willis won the prestigious BP Portrait Award. In addition to the £10,000 prize, she was awarded a commission worth £2,000 to paint a portrait of Lord and Lady Longford for the National Portrait Gallery.

If you are successful in a competition, it's worth using that to get further publicity. Local newspapers and radio are especially interested in such stories. Their angle can seem trivial but it may lead to valuable contacts.

12 • Selling abroad

Selling abroad should be as straightforward as selling in the UK. Other countries can offer better economic conditions, more successful sales outlets and an environment which appreciates and values contemporary visual art and craft.

It's always advisable to have solid experience of selling in this country before dealing with the complexities of overseas shipping, foreign currency and language, export documentation as well as different business cultures. Makers exhibiting at trade fairs often encounter foreign buyers and start to export by chance. Strategic marketing can help develop occasional overseas orders into regular sales.

Research your market

Focus your initial research on one country or region. Where you start may relate to your interests, contacts and skills as much as the market. Consider basic economic indicators which determine whether you could sell your work there at a realistic price. Cost of living rates published in the *Economist* magazine give price comparisons with the UK.

There's a mass of research data on export markets for specific goods in most major countries for consultation in specialist business libraries. You won't find reports solely on visual art and craft but parallel areas, eg fashion, gifts, gardenware, glass can be found. Get a feel for the market in different countries by looking at overseas magazines in the art, craft, design and interiors field. From articles, photographs and advertisements, build up a picture of what people in that country appreciate. The Crafts Council library carries a number of journals giving valuable clues to the visual culture of different countries. Foreign embassies and cultural institutes may also assist with information.

Another less formal research method is contacting makers and artists there direct and asking how and where they sell. Jeweller Diane Hall contacted selected exhibitors at a Paris trade fair to obtain names of agents to sell her work in Europe.

Develop contacts through national organisations of artists and makers and international networks such as the European Textile Network

Paul Berg, *Deep Sea Collection.*
Photo: the artist

**Paul Berg is an Irish artist who
designs and makes furniture.
Brought up in the Netherlands,
he graduated from Rotterdam
Art College and settled in
Dublin in 1988. Paul's work
crosses boundaries between
furniture and sculpture. He
uses a lot of recycled timber,
principally monkey puzzle
which is used as 'wrapping' for
a range of timbers imported
through Dublin Docks and
normally discarded as waste.
His work sells well in Ireland
but with such a small home
market he has to look further
afield: "I get regular orders
from two shop-galleries in the
Netherlands. English galleries
are more difficult because of
sale or return – it's just too
complicated at a distance. The
Crafts Council of Ireland took
my work to Germany in a
showcase of Irish furniture.
They hired a gallery during the
Cologne Furniture Fair. I'm
waiting for orders to come
through as a result."**

and the International Ceramics Academy. Trade information by exchanging lists of outlets and galleries in your respective regions. Such contacts are often best fostered through artists' groups and makers' guilds. Joint projects such as exchange exhibitions an d studio residencies are an excellent starting point for selling your work in that country.

Advice & grants

Learning the language of the export advisory services may be your first foreign language. There is advice and financial assistance available. Such agencies do little to target their information to artists and makers. But once you've convinced them you are a small business seeking to develop overseas markets, expect their support.

Information is available from the DTI, TECs, LECs Rural Development Commission, EuroInfo Centres, Chambers of Commerce, local authority economic development units, Customs and Excise and VAT offices. Some agencies charge for more detailed advice.

Be specific about what you require. Agencies can advise on practicalities such as how to arrange payment,

see 20 • Contracts export documentation and freight forwarders. They cannot answer vague enquiries such as "Will my prints sell in Europe?"

Get the full export information pack from the DTI. Aimed at larger firms, it nevertheless contains useful guidelines for the smaller exporter. They run an Export Desk for each country providing specific information by phone.

Apply for any relevant grants. The DTI and Rural Development Commission offer grants for overseas trade fairs; some local authority

Sally Penn-Smith, *Seaweed*

Sally makes innovative hand-painted 24% lead crystal blown glassware. Her range includes paperweights and perfume bottles. Three years ago when she set up she knew she needed to export to develop her business. Through the DTI 'New Products from Britain' scheme, she promoted her work in the trade press of 15 selected countries. For a reasonable fee, the DTI will write and place a press release in the relevant trade press in any number of countries. Sally finds that UK orders are small and galleries often ask for sale or return whereas export orders are much larger and paid proforma (in advance of dispatch) direct into her bank account in sterling. She sells in Japan, the USA and Saudi Arabia and in 1993 is exhibiting at a major trade fair 'Lifestyle Europe' in Japan.

economic development units offer grants for 'marketing missions' to visit potential buyers in Europe; if you want to develop a partnership project or cultural exchange, you may get help from your RAB; under 26s can apply for a Prince's Trust Go & See grant.

Make contact

You can contact overseas buyers without leaving the country. Make an appointment to show your work to an export buying agent. The EXBO association represents buyers for leading department stores around the world and delivery and payment procedures are very simple.

If your work is visible in the UK, foreign buyers may contact you direct. The Crafts Potters Association Directory is widely used by overseas ceramics buyers.

Selling through an overseas trade fair is a good move for makers with experience of UK trade fairs. Subsidised stands and travel grants are available for some fairs. The New York Gift Fair takes 16 UK makers organised through the Crafts Council with substantial DTI grants. There is great demand for places. You can be subsidised for up to five visits to certain fairs, often necessary since foreign buyers like to see you a number of times before placing an order. East Midlands Arts have organised a group stand for two years at the Frankfurt Messe, a huge trade fair for craftspeople. Erica Just sold a major piece to the owner of a textile gallery based in a castle in Bavaria. She has been promised an exhibition there in 1994.

Makers report a more appreciative environment abroad with trade fair buyers and small gallery dealers willing to purchase work outright. Leaving work on sale or return or consignment overseas presents a real dilemma. If it really is the norm, you may decide to accept it but get your transport costs covered and try to negotiate a deposit. Brian Phillips reports consigning four paintings, worth £940, to a UK-based agent for a promised show in America. In spite of repeated letters and phone calls, he never saw them again. He says: "The experience has closed me in. I feel that I will never deal with agents again."

Your research might lead you to position your work differently for export. Irish furniture-makers exhibiting at the Cologne Furniture Fair found German buyers interested in environmental issues – types and origins of wood and making methods. They concluded that positive marketing of the 'green' qualities of their furniture would enhance its value in the German market.

If you are confident about selling your work direct to shops and galleries, a well-planned sales trip with appointments to visit outlets in a particular country or region can be profitable. Research your contacts and route well. For EC countries, special export documentation is no longer required but get advice on VAT if you are registered (rates vary across the EC) and on documentation for non-EC countries.

See 21 • Further reading, 'Magazines' *Ceramic Review* reported on Alasdair MacDonell's successful sales trip to America. A six week trip resulted in sales to a Hollywood interior decorator, a gallery in Mendocino, California and interested individuals along the way. They left America with "empty luggage, full hearts and minds, confident that there is a huge market there and a receptivity to ideas that fall outside the conventions that often seem to inhibit British ceramics".

Selling abroad

ADVANTAGES
- Access to new and potentially profitable markets.
- Larger orders usually with export.
- Your work may have an exotic appeal to overseas buyers.
- Grants available, especially for trade fairs.
- Contact with artists in other countries brings new ideas and friends.
- A lot of advice and assistance is currently available.

DISADVANTAGES
- Research and selling can be expensive and time-consuming.
- Problems getting paid are greater with overseas sales.
- Competition from other artists and makers who understand the language and culture.
- More complicated doing business in a different language.

13 • Sales administration

It's great to hear people say how much they love your work but no sale is completed until the money is in the bank. If you are serious about selling, it's important to get the paperwork right. Leaving work uncollected in a gallery or failing to verify cheque details means you might as well give it away.

Keeping records

Be absolutely methodical about everything you send out from the studio – work, slides, applications, etc. Write it down and save your memory for more important things.

Card index

This is a good system for recording contacts with shops, galleries, exhibitions and agents. Use large cards, filed alphabetically by outlet. Record the owner's name, address and phone. Each time you are in contact, write down the date and brief details.

You might start with 20 cards for craft galleries and shops you approach with your 'sales package'. Record the date and what you sent (eg slides, CV, postcard) and detail any response and all subsequent contact. It's then a simple task to keep in touch with active selling outlets, making sure you ring them regularly, especially where work is on sale or return. Keep the card box near the phone so you can respond professionally, address gallery owners by name and remind them when you last spoke.

Painter Vicki Cassidy says: "You hear of artists putting work into shows and not knowing what work is due back to them. They've not kept a record. There are some unscrupulous dealers who just say 'they haven't asked me for this painting back so I'll sell it and nobody's any the wiser'. It's a business arrangement. You can't just package up your work, send it to the gallery and assume they'll always be completely straight with you. The artist is as much at fault as the dealer."

Make cards for outlets recommended by other artists. When you want to contact more shops and galleries, follow them up.

Sales invoices & contracts

Always keep a copy of invoices and contracts. You can buy duplicate or triplicate invoice books with carbon sheets. Stamp or write your name and address on it. If you take large numbers of orders, printed self-duplicating forms which can act as Sales Invoice, Reminder, Delivery Note or Order will be useful. Where work is left on consignment or sale or return a contract/receipt is essential. With orders at trade fairs, write details on an order form, confirm payment method, get the buyer's signature and give them a copy. Telephone orders need written confirmation.

Most makers request proforma for first and overseas orders, often with a small discount. You send the proforma invoice to the customer when the work is nearly ready for dispatch. When the customer (shop or gallery) pays and the cheque has cleared, the goods are sent. For overseas orders, direct payment into your bank account (give customers the account number, name and sort code) is a cheaper way of transferring money than foreign currency cheques. There's no guarantee proforma invoices will be paid promptly but it does secure payment in advance and reassures makers dealing with unknown customers.

Orders to regular customers are usually delivered with an invoice. Agree terms of trade with the purchaser and quote them on the in voice. If you quote 'Terms: 30 days', you are giving 30 days credit before payment is due.

VAT

You must register with Customs and Excise if your annual turnover exceeds the VAT threshold, which is £37,600 in the previous 12 months. Once registered you must charge VAT on all chargeable sales and services (17.5% in 1993). Your VAT number must appear on invoices. As a registered business it's essential to keep accurate accounts and file your VAT returns within the specified period. You can reclaim VAT paid on materials and work-related expenditure. Non-payment of VAT due to Customs and Excise is a criminal offence.

For sales through shops and galleries, it's important for artists and makers to understand how VAT is applied. VAT is basically a tax on sales of goods and services. It must be charged by all registered businesses and accounted for to Customs and Excise. Most galleries

An example of the sales paperwork used by Jeweller Jane Adam.

The form is printed in duplicate on self-carbonating paper. Jane Adams says: *"By printing (with a rubber stamp), or writing on, the approprriate heading, I can use it as an order form at trade shows, as an invoice, pro forma invoice, delivery note or statement, or when placing orders with suppliers (deleting the terms and conditions). It adapts easily to these different uses. For instance, the box labelled 'Delivery' can state when an order should be sent, or how the completed order was despatched. Because my orders tend to consist of a selection of several items from a number of ranges, it is useful to have a large box with ruled lines where I can make a clear list.*

Equally, it avoids misunderstanding to have the 'Terms and Conditions' evident on all paperwork."

The form was designed by Jane Adam **and** Nigel Vichi

INVOICE

To				No.	2599	
THE CRAFT GALLERY				Date	7 April 1993	
21, High Street				Your ref.	O|N 265	
London W6 9BJ.				My ref.	J Smith	
				Delivery	Registered post	

Quantity	Ref.	Description		Price	Total
3	AE1	earstuds		7.00	21.00
4	AE2	"		8.50	34.00
2	AE3	" + drops		10.25	20.50
1	AE5	" "			11.50
1	AE8	" "			15.00
2	AB1	brooch		9.00	18.00
2	AP1	pin		6.25	12.50
3	AP2	"		5.00	15.00
1	ZE5	earstuds			18.50
1	ZB3	brooch			22.50
1	ME2f	earstuds			10.00
3	ME4f	" + drops		14.50	29.00
2	MEB8f	brooch		12.00	24.00
					249.50
			+ V.A.T. at 17.5 %		43.66

TERMS: 30 days nett
5% discount for pro forma payment
Pro forma for new customers
Prices exclude delivery and excise
duty, unless otherwise stated

The title of the goods supplied
shall not pass to the customer
until payment has been made
of the full contract price

£ 293.16

J   A   N   E   A   D   A   M

First Floor   27-29 Union Street London SE1 1SD England   071-357 7955   VAT No 480 1342 73

and shops are VAT-registered. Not many artists and makers are, although if you do large commissions, have expensive machinery or work with costly materials you may need to register. If you are not registered it is illegal to charge VAT but quite normal for you to have to pay it on goods and services purchased.

There is a degree of confusion around the charging of VAT on sales of artworks. More outlets make errors through ignorance than intent. When artists sell their work through VAT-registered galleries and shops there are two principles in the application of VAT:

- VAT is always chargeable on the sales commission (the gallery's selling service).
- VAT is also charged on the goods when the artist is VAT-registered or the gallery has bought the work from the artist and is reselling it.

When an outlet acts as an agent, selling work on your behalf, Customs and Excise require a contract between the gallery and artist stating this fact and that the customer understands the arrangement. Use of the sale or return contract/receipt should meet this requirement. If this contractual arrangement is not in order, the gallery must charge VAT on the goods as well as the service (commission) thereby increasing the price.

See 14 • Selling contracts

The following examples show how VAT is charged in different circumstances:

Gallery is VAT-registered but the artist is not

Gallery acts as an agent selling work on behalf of an artist

VAT is only chargeable on the commission. The gallery charges the artist VAT on the selling service element of the price.

Retail price £500.00
Gallery commission (33% of retail) £165.00
VAT on commission (17.5% of 165) £28.88
Total gallery charge £193.88
Artist receives/ trade price £306.12

Gallery buys a work from an artist and resells it

Here the gallery must charge VAT on the full retail price, ie on the goods and the service. All the VAT is charged to the customer who buys the work. The gallery charges the artist the commission rate only. As is usual, when the gallery takes the financial risk of buying work outright, it adds a higher mark-up to the sale.

Retail price inc. VAT £500.00
VAT on retail price (17.5%) £74.47
*Retail price exc. VAT £425.53
Gallery commission (50% of £425.53) £212.76
Artist receives/ trade price £212.76

* To work out the retail price excluding VAT, divide price inc VAT (£500) by 117.5 (= £4.25) and multiply by 100 (retail price = £425.53. £500-£425.53 = £74.47.

It's worth noting in these two examples that, where the artist chooses to fix their retail price, the gallery receives more commission when they buy work outright, but the artist receives more when a work sells on consignment (sale or return). This is because the percentage commission is different – it is quite often the case that a gallery/shop has different commission rates on consignment and outright purchase sales. And this is not the only way to work out your prices. If you prefer to maintain a consistent trade price, the resulting retail price will be substantially higher for outright sales than for consignment sales.

Both gallery and artist are VAT registered

Gallery acts as an agent selling work on behalf of an artist

The gallery on the artist's behalf charges VAT on the full retail price. The gallery charges the artist VAT on the commission element for its selling service.

```
Retail price inc. VAT ....................................£500.00
VAT on retail price (17.5%) .............................£74.47
Gallery commission (33% of 425.53) ...........£140.42
VAT on commission (17.5% of 140.42) .........£24.57
Gallery charges artist (commission + VAT) ...£164.99
Artist receives/trade price ...........................£335.01
```

The artist has to account to Customs and Excise for VAT on the retail price, ie £74.47. The artist can reclaim the £24.57 VAT on behalf of the VAT charged by the gallery. In this situation the gallery collects the VAT on behalf of the artist and bills the customer for it. To avoid the gallery being liable to pay the VAT it collects on behalf of the artist, the artist has to enter into a 'self-billing arrangement' where the gallery is authorised to raise the invoice on behalf of the artist for the sale of the work. The artist then treats the gallery's invoice to the customer as their own VAT invoice. These arrangements have to be agreed by Customs and Excise in advance and most good galleries will have experience of this type of arrangement.

VAT and selling abroad

If you sell to a VAT-registered business in another EC country, you must quote both VAT numbers, with country prefixes (eg UK and FR) on the sales invoice. If you can satisfy these conditions and the supply is of goods then you can zero rate the export from the UK. You must declare such zero rates sales on a European sales listing which has to be sent to Customs and Excise. You must also have proof that you have exported the goods. If you cannot meet these conditions, then sales to the European Community are standard rated. Exports outside the European Community, if you have proof of export, are always zero rated. VAT rates vary across Europe although they are due to be harmonised. Find out whether your work qualifies as a 'work of art' as in some countries these carry a lower rate than other goods.

Getting paid

Cash & cheques

In a high-pressured selling environment such as a market or trade fair, be very organised about taking money. You'll need a cash float but try not to carry large amounts of cash, and bank the takings regularly. If you anticipate large cash takings at a fair, your bank can arrange for you to use a night safe deposit at another branch.

Cheque details need careful scrutiny (signature, date, payee's name, amount). Look at the cheque guarantee card and verify:

• account number

• name

• signature

(all must be the same as on the cheque)

• expiry date (to check card is still valid).

If you have any doubt about the signature, get the customer to sign the back as well and watch them do it. Write the card number (not the account number) and the expiry date on the back of the cheque. For cheques over £50 (some cards guarantee up to £100), ask the customer to write their address on the back and check this against additional identification (eg driving licence).

Credit cards

With direct selling you'll soon find people wanting to pay by credit card. The credit card company charges a percentage fee so there's a cost to this. But the ability to pay by credit card can be a major factor in helping a customer to decide to buy or to spend more on a higher-priced work. Having a credit card facility will be extremely useful at a fair such as Chelsea Crafts Fair.

You'll need Access and Visa. To set up the accounts, ring round the banks to compare deals, convince them of the huge amount of business you'll bring their way and negotiate as low a percentage as possible. You're given a credit limit per sale above which you must ring for authorisation. When making a sale put on the payment slip the customer's name, card number and the date, what is being sold, the price, and possibly the name of the seller (if there is more than one person taking payments). Then get the customer to check this and sign it. Check their signature against the signature on the card. Then give the customer the top sheet (and return their card), and put the rest of the payment slip into your cash box. Pay the slips into your bank, just like cash, and you'll receive a monthly statement from the credit card company saying how much they have debited for the service.

Dail Behennah, *Dish with computer components,* poelut cane, telephone wire & computer components, 61x61x13cms.
Photo: Stephen Brayne **for the Crafts Council**

Dail is a basketmaker living in Bristol who makes to commission and sells through exhibitions and selected galleries and shops. She was delighted when asked to supply baskets to a major London gallery in 1992. They wanted to buy work outright so she agreed to their higher mark-up. Goods were supplied and invoiced but six months later, in spite of letters and phone calls, no payment had been received. Meanwhile, she discovered that two baskets had sold and the gallery mark-up had been increased to 200%. Alarmed by recession stories of gallery closures, she arranged for the unsold work to be removed. Nine months after delivery, after many more phone calls and letters, the threat of court action finally resulted in a post-dated cheque. Dail feels the only way of avoiding this situation was if she'd known of the gallery's poor payment record. This is only possible on an informal basis. Artists and craftspeople are often aware of such reputations in their local area but may not know about galleries further afield.

Special purchase schemes

If your work carries a high price, it's a good idea to sell through outlets operating an art purchase scheme. These offer customers special loans or deferred payment to buy artworks. Studies have shown that these schemes increase sales.

Northern Arts operates its Art Purchase Plan in 35 galleries in the region, offering interest free loans up to £1000 to buy works by living artists. Collectorplan has been running successfully in Welsh galleries for ten years.

Some galleries, shops and individual artists offer less formal arrangements, with payment by instalments, only releasing the work when the last cheque has cleared. The ability to pay in instalments is another incentive to buy but always put the details into a written agreement. A payment schedule should include dates, amounts due and when ownership passes to the purchaser.

Chasing debts

When you start selling regularly you are bound to have money owed to you most of the time. The occasional bad debt is almost inevitable. Your accountant will write it off at the end of the financial year but it is still a loss. Keeping track of what you are owed and chasing it where necessary becomes part of your business activity.

If you have any doubts about supplying a new outlet try and get a credit reference for them, either from their bank or someone else who sells there. A maker reports that all her bad debts have been on second orders. It's all too common for an outlet to agree to pay proforma on the first (small) order, then put in a much larger second order which goes unpaid.

Reminders

With tight cashflow, many businesses only pay against reminders and will resist payment as long as possible. A 1993 study of small businesses in South West England found the average bill was 100 days overdue. It also showed that for every £100 owed by a small business, they were owed £155.

If the credit period of 30 days expires with no payment send a statement. This reminds the customer of invoice details and that payment is now overdue. If you get no response, follow up with a telephone call requesting payment. Direct contact will in most cases result in a cheque but if nothing is forthcoming, send a letter asking for immediate settlement. The third stage is a letter threatening legal action. Keep copies of all letters sent and a record of telephone contact.

Legal action

It's only worth the worry and potential expense of legal proceedings if the size of the debt makes it worthwhile and if you have a reasonable chance of recovering the money. Sometimes it just isn't worth it, and it might make more sense to write off the loss as a bad debt.

A solicitor's letter may get a response in some instances and is always worth trying before taking the matter to court. The small claims section of the county court deals with claims up to £5000. Staff there can advise you. If you win, your legal costs are recoverable from the defendant. Contact your small claims court for advice and then assess whether you think the claim is worth pursuing. If you are using a solicitor check that the solicitor deals in debt cases, and ask for a quote of cost before going ahead or you might be wasting good money chasing a bad debt.

If a gallery goes bust leaving you with outstanding invoices you have up to a month to get your name onto the list of creditors showing that the gallery owes you money. If work is held on sale or return, it still legally belongs to you but you need to inform the liquidators. Otherwise your work may be sold as part of the gallery's assets. Auditors are only obliged to advertise a bankruptcy in the local press so it's very important to keep in touch with your outlets on a regular basis particularly those where you have experienced payment problems.

Angela Edmonds' first solo exhibition was at a London gallery which was repossessed on the night of the private view. What should have been a celebration turned into a nightmare as she tried to reclaim her work. After three days she succeeded. She tried to get compensation for lost sales but eventually realised the case was not worth pursuing.

Problems with overseas outlets may require different solutions. Jane Adam had difficulties getting paid by a US outlet. She managed to recover money with the help of a debt collector but had to pay 25% of the sum recouped in costs.

Insurance liability

You should always seek advice on insurance. Talk to other artists and makers, take advice from any membership organisation you belong to (they may run an insurance scheme), and take advice from an insurance broker. The areas you need to consider are:

- public liability – covers you for accidents to members of the public in your studio or, with an exhibition at a trade fair, etc
- work in transit
- motor insurance – check if your policy covers business use and includes carriage of art works and up to what value
- money – you can cover yourself against loss of cash and cheques in various situations, eg going to the bank
- personal injury and accident
- business interruption – eg loss or damage to equipment preventing you from working
- legal expenses
- contents – protection against fire, theft, damage, etc in the workplace (studio or house), and by extension elsewhere (eg a trade fair). If your studio or workshop is in your house then it is essential that you tell your insurers otherwise your home contents policy may become invalid (you may be able to extend a home contents policy to cover business)
- employers liability – necessary if you employ anyone
- work in exhibitions.

Covering every eventuality can be expensive. You have to weigh up what you can afford and what is essential. But once you have taken out insurance you should review your cover annually and make sure it is still relevant to your needs.

Furniture maker Roger Bateman had a disastrous experience when a leading London gallery involved him in an insurance claim. They sent his piece to be photographed for an interior design magazine feature and reported it returned damaged. Roger travelled to London but estimated the damage as minimal. However the gallery were determined to claim the full value from the magazine's insurance. After three months Roger still hadn't received the £750 owed by the gallery. The piece was on sale or return and would have sold for £1500. Eventually he rang the magazine's accounts department and discovered they paid a £3500 claim to the gallery two months earlier. Further calls and solicitor's letters failed to raise either the £750 payment or his portfolio of slides and photographs. The piece now belonged to the magazine. Finally, in desperation, Roger visited the gallery with a friend and took direct action to reclaim a second piece which the gallery refused to return to him. His advice is to cover yourself on all sides. A contract clause stating that work cannot pass to a third party without the artist's consent would have given him greater legal protection.

14 • Selling contracts

By **Nicholas Sharp**

The chapter is taken from AN Publications *Visual Arts Contracts: Selling* which contains two longer, and more detailed, forms of selling contracts, plus notes.

The contracts, commentary and notes that follow cover one of the commonest legal transactions an artist is likely to encounter – selling work. This could be a studio sale direct to a collector, a sale to a museum or permanent collection, or a sale through a gallery, agent, dealer, or craft shop. What they all have in common is that they involve the sale, to someone else, of a work which before the sale belonged to the artist.

In some cases an agent, gallery or dealer is lent the work to try to sell it, on behalf of the artist. This does not affect the fact that, from a legal perspective, it is the artist who is selling the work. In the case of a studio sale, the artist is selling it him/herself and in the other cases the agent, dealer or gallery is selling the work on behalf of the artist.

This chapter looks at sale transactions and legal consequences of a sale, setting out suggested forms of contract to ensure as far as possible that the artist's position as seller (and usually copyright owner) is protected. It does not attempt to look in detail at any of the specific contracts artists will need when dealing with agents, dealers, galleries or exhibition organisers.

Apart from providing appropriate legal protection, for instance where the buyer, gallery or shop does not pay or goes bust, contracts provide an essential record for preparing your accounts and will help you develop a mailing list of buyers, as well as enabling you to maintain a record of where your work is if you need to borrow it back.

Before using the contracts

The model contracts that follow are designed to be suitable only for simple sale situations. *But they should not be used blindly and artists should check that they are suitable for their specific needs and should always seek legal or other specialised advice if in doubt.* The notes that follow the contract and which are cross-referenced by ➡, in the margin should be read before the contracts are completed. These explain some of the contract wording. AN Publications *Visual Arts Contracts: Selling*, in addition to the contracts that follow, also includes two larger forms of contract with more detailed or specialized provisions

Is there a contract of sale?

Behind every sale, there must be a contract. At some point the seller will have agreed, orally or in writing, to sell the work to the buyer and, provided the basic legal conditions are fulfilled, there will be a contract enforceable in court. *Visual Arts Contracts: An Introduction* includes details of these conditions and emphasises the importance of having written contracts, and not relying on verbal ones. It also includes some guidance on dealing with disputes over contracts, and how to enforce them if things go wrong. All this applies equally to contracts for sale of work. However, there are some specific rules which are especially relevant to selling work:

- As a general rule, no contract will exist unless *the price* has been agreed, or is capable of being determined simply. So if a buyer offers to buy your work, and no price is mentioned, there will be no contract, even if the offer is accepted. If the buyer offers to pay 'up to £500' there is no contract since *the price is not fixed.*

- The work to be sold must be clearly identifiable. If a buyer offers to buy your 'next oil painting' for £500, the work is capable of being identified once it is completed, and so if you accept the offer there will be a contract.

- An offer can always be withdrawn *before* it is accepted. So if a buyer offers £500 for a photographic print, and you do not say you accept it, you are at risk that the buyer will change his/her mind and withdraw the offer.

- If you exhibit a work and show a selling price against it, technically this is *not* an offer, but merely an invitation from you for someone to offer to buy it at that price. What this means is that you (the artist) do not have to accept an offer at the stated price. You may decide for instance not to accept the offer from that particular buyer.

- The law imposes certain terms automatically on every contract for the sale of goods, unless these can be, and are, excluded by agreement between seller and buyer. The most important terms are that the work sold is of 'merchantable quality' and fit for any specific purpose made known by the buyer. These sort of terms could mean that a buyer can claim compensation from you if the work is not properly fabricated or finished. In appropriate cases you can exclude or modify these statutory terms provided this is agreed in writing.

• The terms of a contract must be agreed *on or before* the contract is concluded. Generally speaking, an *invoice* is issued *after* the contract of sale is concluded. What this means is that it is not possible to print contract terms on an invoice and confidently rely on those terms applying. The contract terms must have been made known to, and accepted by, the buyer *when the sale was agreed*.

Nonetheless invoices are useful for tax and record-keeping purposes. Best practice would involve the signing of a contract followed by an Invoice. In this case the invoice might, in addition to the names of seller and buyer, and the work, date and sale price, state '**Subject to terms and conditions of a Contract of Sale dated _____ .**'

Which contract to use?

At this point it is necessary to distinguish between two different situations: the first – **direct sale** – is where you the artist are selling the work yourself, eg a studio sale, an outright sale at a craft fair where you have a stand, a sale to a gallery/shop. The second – **consignment sale** – is where you are lending the work to someone else so that they can sell it on your behalf, eg a dealer, gallery/shop, or by the exhibition organisers as part of an exhibition. This is often known as 'sale or return' but is better called 'consignment sale'. The crucial difference from a direct sale is that with consignment the artist remains the owner of the work until the shop, gallery, dealer, etc sells the work on behalf of (as agent for) the artist. One of the advantages of this is that if the shop goes bust before your work is sold, you will normally be able to reclaim the work and the shop's creditors will not be able to claim it as theirs. But because the work is out of your possession and the sale transaction itself is outside your control, you need to ensure that the contract you have with the shop makes it clear what the shop's responsibilities are.

The contract you need will depend on whether the sale is a direct sale or a consignment sale. The contracts which follow are:

• **Direct Sale Contract**: a short simple form of sale contract for direct sales.

• **Consignment Receipt**: a simple form of consignment agreement for use when works are being lent to a gallery, shop or dealer. This includes the minimum suggested terms for all consignment arrangements.

Direct Sale Contract

Name and address of Artist _____

_____

_____

_____ Tel _____

Name and address of Buyer _____

See notes on
following page:

_____

_____

_____ Tel _____

1 1. **Description of Work and Purchase Price:**
(see attached Appendix for any additional works)

Title _____

Medium _____

Dimensions _____

2 Purchase price £ _____

VAT @ 17.5% £ _____

Total £ _____

(Note: write "N/A" in the VAT space above if the Artist is not VAT registered)

3 2. **Payment Terms:**
Payment to be made in full to the Artist before Work is collected/ delivered. Payment to be by cheque sent to the Artist at the above address.

4 3. **Ownership of the Work** is retained by the Artist until full payment of the purchase-price is made.

5 4. **Copyright:** The Artist retains copyright and all reproduction rights in the Work, unless otherwise agreed in writing by the Artist and the Buyer.

6 5. **Delivery and collection arrangements:** *(give details if applicable)*

Signed (by the Artist) _____

Signed (for and on behalf of Buyer) _____

Date:_____

Notes to Direct Sale Contract

1. **Description of Work**. Any extra works should be listed on a separate **Appendix**.

2. **Purchase Price**. The agreed price must be stated. Value Added Tax: if the artist is VAT registered (currently compulsory if turnover exceeds £37,600 in any period of twelve months or less) then VAT must be added (17.5% – 1993). If the artist is not VAT registered VAT must not be charged. The VAT amount should be shown separately. If not stated, the price always *includes* VAT.

See 13 • Sales administration, 'VAT'

3. **Payment Terms**. It is much wiser to insist on payment in full before the Work is released to the buyer. Credit or instalment sales should be avoided wherever possible. Wording for credit or instalment terms is included in the long form of the direct sales contract in AN Publications *Visual Arts Contracts: Selling*.

4. **Ownership of Work**. This important wording gives the artist the right to reclaim a work if the artist is not paid, provided the buyer still has the Work.

5. **Copyright**. Although under the Copyright Designs and Patents Act 1988, copyright will be retained automatically by the artist unless otherwise agreed in writing, it is better to state this, since buyers are often unaware of the copyright position. If in a particular case it has been agreed that buyer will acquire the copyright or have any reproduction rights, this should be specifically stated in a separate document. Legal advice may be needed. Note that the Act provides that it will not be a breach of the artist's copyright if the buyer reproduces the work for the purpose of advertising the work for sale. This would enable the buyer, whether it is a gallery or a private buyer, to include a reproduction in an exhibition catalogue or postcard, provided this is being done to sell the work.

6. **Delivery/Collection Arrangements**. This should indicate whether the buyer will collect the work and when, or whether the artist is responsible for delivery.

Consignment Receipt

Name and address of Artist _____

_____

_____

_____ Tel _____

Name and address of Gallery/ Shop _____

_____

_____

See notes on   _____ Tel _____

following page: Name of Proprietor _____ Tel _____

1➡ **1.** The Gallery/Shop acknowledges receipt on consignment of the works listed in the attached Appendix: List of Works ("The Works") all in good condition (save as noted in the Appendix). The Gallery/Shop agrees to return any Work unsold in the same condition as received.

2➡ **2.** The Works are consigned to the Gallery/Shop for the purposes of sale only.

3➡ **3.** The Gallery/Shop will sell the Works, as agent for the Artist, at the selling prices set out in the Appendix (which are exclusive of VAT)

4. The Gallery/Shop will be entitled to charge sales commission on the selling prices at the rate specified in the Appendix (plus VAT if applicable)

4➡ **5.** The Gallery/Shop will pay the Artist the selling price less the sales commission (including VAT on the commission if applicable) within _____ days of the date of sale.

5➡ **6.** The Artist retains ownership of the Works until sale.

6➡ **7.** The Artist retains copyright and all reproduction rights.

8. The Artist may withdraw any of the Works on _____ days written notice. The Gallery/Shop may return to the Artist any of the Works on _____ days written notice.

Signed (by the Artist) _____

Signed (for and on behalf of Gallery/Shop) _____

Date: _____

Notes to Consignment Receipt

1. **The Works.** Each work consigned should be listed in an **Appendix** detailing title, medium, dimensions, edition size and number (if applicable), selling price (ie the agreed retail price) from which the commission is deducted and commission percentage. Works added later can be added to the **Appendix**, or a new appendix substituted. In each case the amendments/new appendix should be signed by both parties. The appendix should also contain an acknowledgement that the works were received by the gallery/shop in good condition, to avoid later arguments.

2. **Purpose and Scope of Agency.** This makes it clear that the gallery/shop only has authority to keep the work for sale purposes, and not as part of some wider agency or representative role. This means that the gallery/shop cannot claim commission on other works or on studio sales. If the gallery/shop wants to have agency over some or all of your other works, a different type of contract will be needed (this will be dealt with in a later Visual Arts Contract).

3. **Selling Prices and Commission and VAT.** The agreed retail selling prices (excluding VAT) are to be stated in the **Appendix**. The agreed sales commission should be stated in the **Appendix** and may be deducted by the gallery/shop from the selling price.

See 13 • Sales administration, 'Chasing debts'

4. **Payment Terms.** You will need to agree the payment terms with the gallery/shop. 30 days would be a fair starting point from an artist's point of view since most businesses do monthly accounts.

5. **Ownership of Work.** This is important. It provides that you remain the owner of the work until it is sold; the gallery/shop is acting as your agent, so never owns the work. This means that if the gallery/shop goes bust, it is more difficult for creditors to claim your work; the gallery/shop never owns it.

6. **Copyright.** You will retain copyright and if the gallery/shop wants any specific reproduction rights it must get your written approval. This should be done in a separate document; the important point is to be specific about what reproductions are allowed, whether you will receive any payment, and whether you need to approve the quality. Note that under the Copyright Designs and Patents Act 1988, the gallery/shop will be entitled to reproduce the work for the purpose of *advertising its sale*, even without your permission. But this doesn't enable the gallery/shop to sell postcards or catalogues without your consent once the work is sold.

Using the contracts

The contracts and notes above are intended to give guidance and advice of a general nature. The advice of a solicitor or other expert should always be sought for specific situations. While every effort has been made to give accurate and up-to-date information, neither the author nor AN Publications can accept liability for errors or omissions.

With every contract used:

- Both parties should sign the contract (and any Appendix) in duplicate and date both copies.
- The artist should keep one copy and give the other to the other party.
- The contract should be signed *on or before* the delivery of the work to the buyer or shop, gallery or dealer.

Artist

'Artist' has been used throughout as a shorthand to include fine artists, photographers and craftspeople.

15 • Selling & the law

Sales legislation

As the maker and seller of your work you have a legal obligation to comply with laws designed to protect both you and the purchaser.

Relevant legislation includes the Sale of Goods Act 1979, Trades Descriptions Act, Consumer Protection Act and Supply of Goods and Services Act. You can study them in detail in a public library.

You have a legal obligation to supply goods of "merchantable quality" which fit the purpose described. Makers must describe their work accurately to avoid problems. A textile hanging which is delicate and purely decorative should not be described as a rug. Makers of garden pots take care when describing them as frost resistant. It's better to err on the side of caution and not claim work has a function which it cannot fulfil.

Make sure any labels and instruction leaflets which accompany work sold comply with sales legislation. Be careful about cleaning instructions and use any international symbols accurately. If selling work abroad, you may have to provide a translation of instructions where they are necessary for the assembly or use of the piece.

Specialist regulations

The Trading Standards Department at the county or borough council has officers who give free advice on specific regulations. However, one maker reports being charged for information and says you are likely to be inspected as soon as they know you exist. It may be preferable to seek advice from other artists or a membership organisation first.

In the EC many regulations are the same in all countries. But differences still exist. Consumer protection laws are most stringent in the USA where additional standards exist for most products. Get specialist advice when selling abroad.

Toys

Anything sold as a toy must meet specific safety standards. These may also apply to decorative objects which could be mistaken for a toy.

The Blue Cat Toy Company who make hand-made rubber stamps have experienced the full range of legal requirements for toys. The familiar 'CE' mark, now required for toys supplied to children under 14, means that every element of the product (wood, rubber, glue, paint) has been tested by an official test house for a fee of £30 – £40 per test. Separate tests are required for every new batch number (eg of paint) although companies can guarantee their product with a 'Certified Paint Statement'. Toys with small parts must be labelled as unsuitable for children under three. The product must carry the maker's name and address.

See 20 • Contracts, 'Professional organisations'
The British Toymakers Guild has campaigned on behalf of craftspeople making one-off and small run designs to simplify the testing and certification procedures. They have produced a booklet, *EEC Toy Safety Directive 1990: a guide to self-certification.*

Ceramics

One of the concerns for makers of domestic ceramics is lead glazes. Trading standards officers are familiar with metal release standards. They test the amount of lead leaching out of the glaze using a vinegar solution which dissolves it. The British Ceramic Research Institute advises against making glazed ceramic vinegar bottles. In the USA regulations are vigorously enforced following cases of lead poisoning from ceramic mugs.

Electrical goods

From late 1993, new regulations oblige the maker to put a plug and wiring diagram onto electrical goods, eg metal and stained glass lamps.

Jewellery

The Hallmarking Act is extremely rigorous in its legal protection for makers and purchasers of gold, silver and platinum objects. Information on the Act and registration is available from the Assay Office.

Problems arise for jewellers combining metals in an experimental way. If your design incorporates precious and base metals, any gold part must be described as "yellow metal", silver or platinum as "white metal". This causes difficulties for jewellers making high quality pieces with gold or silver fittings which cannot be labelled or described as such. A customer allergic to all but gold ear ring posts will not understand when you say they are "yellow metal". But large fines are a real deterrent to breaking hallmarking legislation.

Copyright

Copyright law protects the artist from unauthorised reproduction of their work. It asserts the artist's ownership of the exclusive right to reproduce it unless copyright is transferred to another person. Copyright is not transferred when a work is sold.

The law covers "artistic works" and "works of artistic craftsmanship". Craftspeople seeking to establish their rights may have to define their intention in the making of a piece. A purely functional piece may not be covered by copyright but may be protected under design right.

Copyright protection lasts for the artist's life plus 50 years unless the work has been industrially exploited (eg a bowl being manufactured in bulk). Design right normally applies for ten years from the first marketing of the design.

The use of the copyright symbol "©" is not required in the UK or in most countries in the world bound by an international convention. However, it is recommended as a reminder of who actually owns the copyright. Artists are advised to use it with their name and date of work's creation on slides registered with slide indexes, postcards and, where appropriate, on the back of original works, and so on.

Apart from transferring copyright ownership, an artist can licence someone else to reproduce their work. The contract can limit reproduction to a period of time, a certain number of copies or specific purposes. Copyright licences can be a useful way for an artist to make income from their work. Rather than selling work outright, they sell the right to make a print, card or poster of it. Some outlets will find it more profitable to sell an image in quantity and regularly negotiate copyright licences (eg a poster only for sale through one chain of shops). The artist receives either a flat fee or royalties which can over time amount to more than the value of the original work.

The Design and Artists Copyright Society (DACS) is a non profit-making society formed by artists in 1984 to administer and protect the copyright in all visual artists' work. DACS protects artists' copyright by actively pursuing unauthorised reproductions of their members' work and, where appropriate, taking up their cases in law. It issues copyright licences and has established reciprocal agreements with similar societies worldwide. Membership is open to all visual artists who can join DACS on payment of a one-off fee.

Trade marks

You can use a symbol or signature as a trade mark to identify work made by you. It is possible to register your mark with the Patent Office although this is a slow and expensive procedure and unlikely to be of practical use to most artists and makers.

16 • Effective promotion

Promotion is the fourth element of your marketing strategy (the four 'p's of product, place, price, and promotion) and is the way you communicate with your market. Time invested in promoting yourself and your work can really pay off in terms of increased sales.

What you need to promote yourself
Any artist or maker seeking to promote themselves starts with a commitment to making their work. As you commit yourself to making a living from it, try to develop a positive, confident manner when describing your work. If you enjoy talking about it and can communicate this pleasure to the listener, you've got a head start in the business of promotion. Slowly you build up a range of 'promotional tools' such as:

• portfolio
• CV
• slides and photographs
• business cards
• headed paper
• postcards
• leaflets
• catalogues (for exhibitions and buyers)
• labels and special packaging
• press folder with editorial cuttings and reviews.

You'll start with the basics – CV, portfolio, some slides and photographs. Invest in others as you need them. Spend as much as you can afford to produce good quality promotional tools. Ask other artists and makers for recommendations of photographers and postcard printers. Look at examples and compare price quotes. Collect examples of design and layout for inspiration.

Painter Carole Waller is realistic in stating "not having much self-confidence or money, artists often can't afford to be as professional as

REPTILE
tiles & ceramics

Carlo Briscoe
&
Edward Dunn
494 Archway Road
Highgate
London N6 4NA
Tel: 081 341 4908

Reptile **are a young ceramics partnership,** Carlo Briscoe **and** Edward Dunn**, who produce an exciting, colourful range of handmade and majolica tiles.**

They decided to produce a full colour A4 folded leaflet which features a number of their designs. "We knew we needed to promote ourselves better. At the time it was a difficult decision to spend money on a full colour leaflet – it cost us £1000 and we had to borrow the money. But it's been amazing. Our turnover has doubled and I reckon we've had over £25,000 worth of work directly as a result of that leaflet. Someone picked it up at Chelsea Crafts Fair by chance. They then showed it to the developers of four new Waitrose supermarkets who have commissioned four large tile panels from us. If they hadn't taken our leaflet, we would never have got that job."

they need to be in their early days. I've learned through experience that the cheap option isn't always a good solution."

Ceramicist Sally Bourne describes the information she sent buyers when she first started. "I cringe to look at it now. I can understand why they said they weren't interested. You've got to get out, be seen, create a professional atmosphere around yourself before people are really interested."

Try to get a consistent style and quality in all your promotional material. You don't need a corporate logo or expensive graphic designer to achieve a clean simple style. Aim to bring all your promotional tools up to the standard of the best of them. Once you've got a smart full colour leaflet, your CV produced on a friend's typewriter with handwritten amendments starts to look distinctly scrappy. It could be greatly improved at little cost by being redesigned on a computer and laser-printed, maybe picking out those 'achievements' you think will interest a particular reader. You can then have several different versions.

One of the keys to successful marketing is understanding the 'benefits' your product offers the customer. Your promotional material must clearly convey these benefits, both in words and image. If subtle colour washes are a feature of your paintings, a cheaply-printed postcard will not do them justice. Remember to include on your CV your sales outlets and work purchased for collections as well as exhibitions. Purchasers of contemporary artworks often lack confidence in matters of taste and aesthetic judgement so the fact that you sell through a certain shop or gallery can help reassure them of the value of your work.

Press

Press coverage, whether exhibition reviews, editorial features in interior design magazines or local press articles, offers excellent free publicity. You almost always have to invest time to gain media attention but you don't actually pay for it.

Plan your approach well in advance. Find out what the publication's deadline is. The last date for you to get information in varies from a few days for a local paper or listings magazine to several months for a glossy magazine. When commissioning photographs of a seasonal event, some interiors and style magazines actually work up to a year ahead of publication.

Editorial features

In terms of selling your work, the best press which undoubtedly leads to sales interest for makers (and many visual artists), is a photograph of your work and brief description in one of the glossy interiors or style magazines. *Country Living, Homes and Gardens, Elle Decoration* and others have regular features. Anything new and beautiful which appeals to their readers is included – paintings and prints, glass, ceramics, jewellery, hand-bound books, etc. Write to the Features or Shopping Editor (name in the magazine), they are always interested in hearing from artists and makers. Make it easy for them by providing excellent quality visuals, preferably large format transparencies, and write something short and suitably flowery about you and your work. Look at current magazines for examples.

A small feature in *Country Living* resulted in orders worth £2000 for the Blue Cat Toy Company. Gavin Rookledge reported lots of enquiries and orders when his handbound books featured in the same magazine. All sales are mail order so make sure your prices include post and packing.

Magazines use artists' and makers' work in photographic features for style, fashion, food and interior sections. Props buyers and set stylists are always looking out for new ideas and objects. They visit trade fairs, buy work direct from makers and should arrange transport to the

Deborah Lawrence, *Boy and Dog*

Deborah set up as a photographer in Manchester under the Enterprise Allowance Scheme in 1992. She produces work to commission for newspapers, magazines and charitable organisations as well as developing a personal project, documenting religious faith and festivals. Through winning a Prince's Trust awards scheme for under 26s, she came to the attention of the British Council in Manchester who sponsored an exhibition of her work in the stunning atrium of their headquarters. The exhibition, 'Face to Face', featured portraits of the people of Hulme, an area just five minutes away. It was timed to coincide with a full board meeting and the Assistant Director-General's retirement party. Both events brought large numbers of influential people into the building to view the exhibition. Deborah was featured in the Manchester Evening News and interviewed on BBC GMR local radio. She has developed contacts with a freelance journalist and hopes to tour the exhibition throughout the Manchester area.

photographer's studio for larger pieces on loan. Such coverage is excellent publicity. You get good quality reproductions of your work in a stylish environment. Glossy magazines have huge readerships and their recommendation of your work can be more valuable than paid advertising.

Press releases

Other press coverage may be less directly related to sales but all contributes to your promotion as an artist. You can easily develop the skill of writing a press release to get coverage of an exhibition or special event.

It must be concise (one side of A4) and typed with double-spaced lines. Put the date at the top and your name, phone number and address for information at the end. Include the following:

• Who (name of artist, organisation)

• What (event, programme, exhibition)

• Where (place)

• When (date and time)

• Why (the intention behind the event).

Seize the journalist's attention in the first two lines and don't clutter the release with jargon, long words or detailed descriptions. Send your press release, in good time, to your targeted press list and follow up with a phone call. If you can offer good quality black-and-white photographs, local newspapers will often respond more readily. The advantage of printed media is that you keep a copy for your press folder but radio and television are another good way of putting your message across and may reach more people. It is often a good idea to phone before you send a press release to find out who to send it to and what sort of information they want.

Keep all press cuttings in a folder. Magazines may send you extra 'tear sheets' on request so you have spare copies for favoured customers.

Event listings

See 21 • Further reading, 'Magazines' Free listings (in local newspapers, event magazines, *Arts Review, Art Monthly,* and other specialist magazines) are ideal for publicising exhibitions and special sales. Check the copy date and send your information, concisely written in listings form, clearly indicating which issues it should appear in. Include a press release to encourage additional coverage. It's a good idea to send information in well in advance of the event – if the details are printed wrong a week early, you've got time to ring in with corrections.

Overseas coverage

If you are planning to do an overseas trade fair, press coverage in the country's design or trade press will be extremely helpful, especially where another language is spoken. Plan ahead and take advantage of the DTI's Export Promotion scheme 'New Products from Britain' to reach the local trade press.

Advertising

Paid advertising is a form of direct communication with your market. Research the readership of the publication and costs before committing yourself. Special advertising sections for Christmas, themes or regional features may appeal but advertising is generally expensive. Fully exploit free listings and editorial features before considering it.

Talks & demonstrations

A valid form of advertising and self-promotion, talks offer the rare opportunity to bridge the gap between the artist and the work, both for maker and viewer. Always offer to give a talk, slide show or demonstration to accompany an exhibition. Show the full range of your work and mention your price range (it encourages the audience to value it). You may be there to demonstrate technique or discuss your inspiration but do also talk about how you make a living as an artist. People are always interested and it can help dispel myths about artists' lives. If you take a portfolio, print bin or small range, you may get some sales. Offer an

Anna Warsop, *Park*, monoprint

"When I've sold work through the Royal Academy Summer Exhibition, they give you the buyers' addresses for you to send work. I dispatched each print enclosing four photographs of other work with prices, my CV and a letter inviting them to contact me if they wanted to see more. About 20% responded and I sold a lot as a result. A London doctor showed the photos round at dinner parties and I sold 20 prints. All his friends wanted them for their waiting rooms. To begin with I was quite worried about approaching people like this but it's not a hard sell. They were genuinely interested and it was an easy way for them to buy artwork."

handout or postcard with your name and details so you can be contacted later.

Looking after your customers

This is essential public relations for everyone who sells their work. Always respond immediately and politely to a customer's complaint and do your best to put it right. It's in your interest to know, for example, if you're using the wrong glue and work is falling apart in use. So be thankful you've been alerted to the problem and sort it out promptly.

Jane Adam sees it as good PR: "I will always mend a damaged or broken piece and never charge for it. By responding well to a customer's complaint, I've got a satisfied customer. They'll be pleased now."

Mailing lists

Direct selling offers a real advantage over gallery and shop sales in that you know who your customers are. Keep their names and addresses and build up a mailing list. Divide your lists into private and trade buyers. Anyone who has bought your work is far more likely to buy it again than the unknown customer.

Invite them to your shows by sending personal invitations. In the business world, mailing lists are sold. Consider trading customer names with someone whose work complements yours without being in direct competition. A joint show or sale offers the opportunity of doubling your mailing list and customers.

17 • Reviewing your progress

It's vital in any business to make time to stand back and review your progress. Part of your marketing strategy was setting yourself a goal of selling more successfully through a number of defined objectives. Looking at what you have achieved will help you appreciate your successes and be clearer about the way forward.

When to review?

An annual review is a good idea. Remember, you set yourself objectives which you aimed to achieve over a specific period. January is often an appropriate time for planning the year ahead. The end of your financial year when you review your annual accounts may suit others. It's important not to choose a time of the year when you are busy or lacking in energy and optimism.

Sometimes people reach a point of desperation when it feels as though the business is controlling them. Success early in your career when everyone is demanding your work, you start cutting corners and begin to hate making it can lead to such a crisis. That's the time to stand back, review the situation and regain control of the business yourself.

Ceramicist Sally Bourne describes the process: "You have to keep stopping and readjusting your aim, as it were. You're constantly pulling yourself up and reassessing things. I'm always thinking, how can I better this? There's no point slogging your heart out. You'll only end up hating the art because it's grinding you into the ground. If you can keep a bit of that satisfaction and enjoyment and turn it into something that can actually make money, you can get a lot more enjoyment out of it. I do find I need to take control from time to time."

An annual review is when you consider the wider business picture. It's a part of your business plan. But throughout the year it's important to remain flexible and alert to new selling opportunities. Do feel able to review your activities as necessary.

What to consider?

Look at your activity over the past year under the following headings:

Product

What have you made? What has sold best? Have you developed any new ranges or types of work? Is there something new you want to develop which needs time, machinery or expertise? Could you get help making the work?

Price

What price work has sold best? Any price ranges you want to drop? Look at your annual accounts to work out your hourly rate. Is it sufficient?

Place

Where have you sold work? (List types of outlets plus different countries.) Which places offer potential for increased sales? Which places have you enjoyed selling to? Which places have caused problems (eg difficulties with payment)?

Promotion

What promotional material have you developed over the year? Any examples of good publicity? Any contacts from trade shows or exhibitions to follow up? Could you get help promoting the work?

Other areas

Other areas for review include looking at the objectives you set yourself. Did you achieve them? If not, did you allow enough time, were they too ambitious or have they become less important in light of other events? The annual review is the time to consider what directions to take over the next year. Set yourself new objectives and remember the SMART principle.

See 3 • Making marketing work for you,'Stage 3: Your objectives'

The SWOT analysis is worth looking at one year on. What has changed? Have you developed new activities and experience which add to your Strengths? Are there changes in market conditions which constitute new Opportunities or Threats?

Make the review process enjoyable and translate your findings into visual stimuli which interest and encourage you. Some makers like to have a map with coloured pins marking their outlets. Graphs and charts of sales figures belong in the business world but may be what you need to visually remind you of your progress.

Getting advice

It's always a good idea to get support and an objective eye when reviewing your activities. You may already have a business adviser through the Prince's Youth Business Trust, Livewire, a business enterprise

Frannie **is a textile designer making dazzlingly colourful painted silk ties, scarves, braces, earrings and waistcoats.**

She sells successfully through trade fairs, department stores, galleries and shops. She exports, particularly to the USA, where the exclusive Neiman Marcus catalogue features her work. "I've reached the stage where I know I've got to get bigger. I feel I've really achieved something working for myself. I work for myself because I have a lifestyle I like. And I don't want it to get too pressurised. I honestly can't work out whether I'm actually happy like this or just scared of expanding."

centre, etc. If you attend a marketing course, ask about a follow-up seminar to review your strategy.

Specialist advice is available from Export Development Advisers through the DTI. They can help review your export activity to date and advise on which areas offer potential.

Success = growth?

Standard business practice equates growth with success. But for artists and makers, defining success is more complex. In pursuing increased sales, you may find you have left little time for experimentation and development. Some of the freedom and enjoyment of being an artist can be lost if you don't maintain that balance.

A maker describes her experience: "I reached the point after my first 18 months when I was working all the hours God sends. I wasn't enjoying it, and had no time to develop. I wanted to give up because I was too successful. I was just too busy. And I decided the answer was either putting the prices up so I was making less, employing people to do stuff for me, buying machinery to make it quicker to do or sending work out to be finished. The answer was to do all of them."

Once you can manage all the different aspects to earning a living from your work and begin to really enjoy the selling and business side as well as the making, there is a great satisfaction from running your own business. A degree of self-sufficiency is part of that. Making decisions about expanding the business can make you question your aims. Sound advice is essential at this point. Sorting out what you want to gain from the business involves personal satisfaction and self-development as well as sales success.

18 • Training

The training needs of self-employed artists and makers are becoming more acknowledged. It's worth considering a course to improve your selling and marketing skills. Few offer formal qualifications but this is changing through adoption of nationally agreed standards. In future, courses may offer students NVQs, a validated qualification accepted across Europe.

The best courses include input from artists and makers who are currently successfully selling their work. If you have experience, offer your skills as a tutor.

Artists Newsletter Information Service is building up a database of short courses of relevance to artists, photographers and makers. It's worth looking in the magazine's listings section to see what is currently on offer.

Art & design colleges
Traditionally tutors have done little to enlighten art students about the realities of selling their work and earning a living after graduation. This is changing and students might want to consider this before applying for courses.

Ask whether business and professional studies are included. Are there visiting tutors with experience of selling their work today?

A half-day business seminar in the final term is insufficient it is consistent attention that demonstrates a college's commitment to teaching students how to make a living from their art. For example, Roger Bateman teaches business studies to artists and designer-makers at Liverpool Institute and finds students eager to learn. The BTEC HND in Design Crafts at Herefordshire College of Art and Design is supported by regular visits from practising makers and gallery owners. At the degree show, a special buyer's session gives graduating students contact with the market and results in considerable sales success.

Enterprise programmes

With a broad brief to provide business advice and counselling, consultancy and training for small businesses, local Training and Enterprise Councils (TECs) support a range of initiatives. TECs (LECs in Scotland) administer the government-sponsored Enterprise Allowance Scheme which operates under different names around the country. This scheme and courses organised by training providers to the TEC may be open to all local businesses or be designed for those starting up.

In some large cities, the TECs sponsor business and marketing courses specifically designed for artists and makers. In 1992 the Manchester TEC sponsored a 22 week Arts Programme for "painters, sculptors, craft or fashion designers". The course, open to people registered unemployed for at least six months, offered training in marketing, promotion, selling methods, finance and sponsorship. In 1993 AN Publications ran some courses with funding from the TEC's Business Enterprise Programme (BEP). In contrast to most BEPs these were solely for artists and makers and were founded on the notion that you learn quickly (and retain information) with a group of like-minded people and a trainer who speaks from experience.

General courses for new businesses on the other hand bring together people working in completely different fields. Glass designer Sally Penn-Smith is enthusiastic about the course she did at Durham University Business School. The course was free under the Graduate Enterprise Programme and she received a training allowance. "I found the tutors very open and interested. They admired me for wanting to make a living as an artist. I know that I wouldn't have got anywhere if I hadn't done that course. Now I teach on it as well as making a living from selling my work."

London Enterprise Agency run the Business Planning Programme over eight weekends with a two-day block devoted to issues specific to art and design businesses.

Arts management organisations

Arts management training units exist in Edinburgh, Newcastle, Leicester, Liverpool, Brighton and Bristol aiming to service training needs of artists and arts organisations. Relevant courses have included 'Marketing for Artists and Craftspeople', held in 1992 in Liverpool and 'Developing your Crafts Business', a two day seminar in Leicester. If no courses are available in your region, your RAB may offer assistance with fees and travel.

RABs are a source of information on short training courses. They may sponsor Selling or Marketing courses in their region. East Midlands Arts organised 'Trading Places' in 1993, to bring makers into contact with

115

European gallery buyers and learn how to present their work to that market. Other RABs offer occasional practical courses in photographing your work, press and publicity, etc. If as an artist or maker you have a particular training need, let your RAB know. It takes time to finance and organise a course but if sufficient people request assistance, they may be able to respond.

Miscellaneous training opportunities

Small businesses in rural England may benefit from marketing courses organised by the Rural Development Commission. Contact your local office as each runs a different programme. Elsewhere, the Welsh Development Agency, Scottish Enterprise and LEDU in Northern Ireland may offer advice and promote training.

A few adult education institutes run relevant courses, usually extremely popular. In London, the City Lit has a one year course for illustrators, developing a portfolio and learning how to get work. Tutor Carmel Hayes says students come from all fine art and design backgrounds. Kensington and Chelsea College run a 'Ceramics Exhibition Course'. Students prepare work for exhibiting and selling with lectures on "marketing, selling and how to survive as an independent artist".

Learning from others

A completely informal level of training exists where artists and makers learn from each other. If you are a student or recent graduate considering setting up, it's well worth negotiating some form of 'apprenticeship' with an experienced artist or maker. It's up to you to sort out the terms and conditions. What is certain is that, even if you spend time doing basic tasks, you can learn an enormous amount. You might find yourself preparing materials, finishing or packing work, assisting at a trade fair, listening to how they deal with orders or organising transport for work. You'll learn a great deal very quickly and confront the reality of making a living as an artist.

19 • Financial assistance

Grants are available to artists and makers for training, promotional materials, marketing initiatives and trade fair attendance. Some organisations also offer loans. Read the guidelines carefully and present your application well. It's not worth applying if you don't meet the criteria.

Commercial or cultural?

Arts agencies are broadly concerned with creative development and may reject purely commercial applications. Business enterprise agencies support business growth and job creation and may view artists as not commercially viable. However, cultural agencies do support some selling and marketing activities, understanding that artists can only develop if they make a living from their work. And, in times of high unemployment, government agencies are forced to acknowledge that even one-person artist or craftsperson businesses can be viable.

Travel grants

Useful both for marketing activity (attending a trade fair, visiting local galleries, etc) and creative development (research, new inspiration, contact with local artists). If possible, combine the two. Your grant might be to focus on one but try to include time to explore the other.

Banks

If you need to raise money to buy equipment or convert workshop space, the bank may be your first stop. Most banks have Small Business Advisers and they will want to see a business plan and cash flow. You may need a loan or to negotiate overdraft facilities to cover periods when you want to buy materials or services but have not yet received payment for your goods. It's advisable to shop around for the best terms. Don't forget that bank charges and interest payments are permitted business expenditure and can be offset against tax in your accounts.

Your selling skills will be needed when approaching the bank. They may be sceptical and need convincing that you are making something that people will buy. Be positive about what you do and talk confidently about your 'product' in the business language they are familiar with.

Regional arts boads & arts councils

See 20 • Contacts, 'Regional arts boards & arts contacts'

RABs in England, the Welsh Arts Council, Scottish Arts Council and Arts Council of Northern Ireland all have specialist programmes of support. Contact your local Visual Arts or Crafts Officer for details. For example, grants may cover exhibitors at Chelsea Crafts Fair, travel bursaries (including researching new markets), training grants and promotional material.

As well as financial assistance, such organisations provide useful information. Some produce a regular newsletter, normally free to artists in the region, with opportunities and news. Ask for information sheets on, for example, shops and galleries in the region, marketing courses and recommended artwork photographers. Some produce relevant publications. Many maintain slide indexes and directories of artists and makers and promote them to public art commissioners. Some purchase work direct from artists in their area, eg Scottish Arts Council and South East Arts, who maintain contemporary collections.

The Crafts Council offers setting up grants to makers in England and Wales. They run a non-selective Register of Makers and an Index of Selected Makers. The latter is used by "architects, designers and others wishing to commission one-off pieces, by shops and galleries seeking to acquire unusual, saleable stock". They organise Chelsea Crafts Fair and co-ordinate group stands with DTI support at selected overseas trade fairs.

Programmes for under 26s

Prince's Youth Business Trust (PYBT)

See 20 • Contacts, 'Business & advisory services'

Financial and other assistance for 18-25s setting up in business. As well as grants and loans, invaluable help and advice comes from the business adviser scheme. An adviser appointed to your business can help you draw up a marketing plan and encourage you to pursue your objectives. PYBT supports many craftspeople and artists setting up in business. It provides marketing opportunities to businesses through group stands at trade fairs and exhibitions such as Ideal Home, Chelsea Flower Show, ArtMart and the Clothes Show.

It also organises an annual PYBT Showcase, in 1992 at the NEC Birmingham International Autumn Fair. Selected businesses receive substantial subsidy to attend.

Livewire
Cash awards, business advice and support for 16-25s starting up in business. A network of coordinators based at enterprise agencies and local authorities promote the scheme. The Business Growth Challenge offers high quality management training to owner-managers of small businesses, aged up to 30, through business counselling and a residential weekend event. 1992 business start-up award winners included a furniture designer and glass artist.

Partners in Europe (The Prince's Trust)
For under 26s wanting to develop a project or business idea with partners in other European countries. Go and See grants of up to £500 cover travel, accommodation and other expenses. Successful projects aim to provide mutual benefit to both partners. A new grant programme for 1993 includes selling and business trips to Europe.

Other agencies
DTI
A range of export and overseas promotion schemes, eg subsidy for exhibiting at overseas trade fairs (generally 50% costs plus travel grant). Other advisory services may be free or subsidised. You can arrange for someone from your local office to come and visit you.

Rural Development Commission
Assistance for small businesses based in villages and small towns in England with less than 10,000 inhabitants. Offer marketing consultancy grants (50% of costs to a maximum £1000) to employ a consultant to plan a marketing strategy. Exhibition grants (50% to a maximum £500) help small rural firms rent space at trade shows or exhibitions.

Local authorities
Some operate export promotion schemes through their Economic Development Unit, eg grants for marketing trips or trade fair attendance to develop business in Europe. Criteria may include potential for business growth and job creation to improve the local economy.

Grant-making trusts

The guiding principles of charitable trusts are education and welfare. Grants are usually made to organisations rather than individuals. The few trusts open to applications from artists and craftspeople generally advertise in *Crafts* and *Artists Newsletter.* A straight commercial proposal for selling and marketing work rarely meets their criteria.

The Winston Churchill Travelling Fellowships offer bursaries covering travel and living expenses for a stay of about eight weeks in another country. Applicants propose a study project related to their trade, profession or interests. Special categories are determined each year. In 1992, grants were offered to "Designers and Craftsmen in Jewellery and Precious Metals".

20 • Contacts

Arts and craft councils

Arts Council of Great Britain (ACGB), 14 Great Peter Street, London SW1P 3NQ tel 071 333 0100

Arts Council of Ireland, 70 Merrion Square, Dublin 2 tel (010 353) 1 611840

Arts Council of Northern Ireland, Stranmillis Road, Belfast BT9 5DU tel 0232 381591

British Council, Visual Arts Department, 11 Portland Place, London W1N 4EJ tel 071 930 8466

Crafts Council, 44a Pentonville Road, London N1 9BY tel 071 278 7700

Crafts Council of Ireland, HQ, South William St, Dublin 2 tel (010 353) 1 6797368

Scottish Arts Council, 12 Manor Place, Edinburgh EH3 7DD tel 031 226 6051

Welsh Arts Council, Museum Place, Cardiff CF1 3NX tel 0222 394711

Regional arts boards

Eastern Arts Board (Bedfordshire, Cambridgeshire, Essex, Hertfordshire, Lincolnshire, Norfolk, Suffolk) Cherry Hinton Hall, Cherry Hinton Road, Cambridge CB1 4DW tel 0223 215355

East Midlands Arts Board (Leicestershire, Northamptonshire, Nottinghamshire, Derbyshire excluding High Peak District) Mountfields House, Forest Road, Loughborough LE11 3HU tel 0509 218292

London Arts Board (Greater London) Elme House, 133 Long Acre, London WC2E 9AF tel 071 240 1313

Northern Arts Board (Cleveland, Cumbria, Durham, Northumberland, Tyne & Wear) 9-10 5Osborne Terrace, Jesmond, Newcastle upon Tyne NE2 1NZ tel 091 281 6334

North West Arts Board (Lancashire, Cheshire, Merseyside, Greater Manchester, Derbyshire High Peak District) 12 Harter Street, Manchester M1 6HY tel 061 228 3062

Southern Arts Board (Berkshire, Buckinghamshire, Hampshire, Isle of Wight, Oxfordshire, Wiltshire, East Dorset) 13 St Clement Street, Winchester SO23 9DQ tel 0962 855099

South East Arts Board (Kent, Surrey, East & West Sussex) 10 Mount Ephraim, Tunbridge Wells TN4 8AS tel 0892 515210

South West Arts Board (Avon, Cornwall, Devon, Gloucestershire, Somerset, Dorset excluding Bournemouth, Christchurch & Poole) Bradninch Place, Gandy Street, Exeter EX4 3LS tel 0392 218188

West Midlands Arts Board (Hereford and Worcester, Shropshire, Staffordshire, Warwickshire, West Midlands) 82 Granville Street, Birmingham B1 2LH tel 021 631 3121

Yorkshire & Humberside Arts Board (Humberside, North, South and West Yorkshire) 21 Bond Street, Dewsbury WF13 1AX tel 0924 455555

Business and advisory services

Assay Office, Goldsmith's Hall, Gutter Lane, London EC2V 8AQ tel 071 606 8975. Information on hallmarking regulations.

Export Buying Offices Association (EXBO), Londwood, Cadogan Pier, Chelsea Embankment, London SW3 5RQ

Department of Trade and Industry (DTI) In England, see Yellow Pages for your regional office. Elsewhere DTI services operated by The Scottish Office, The Welsh Office and Industrial Development Board for Northern Ireland.

LEDU (Small Business Agency for Northern Ireland), LEDU House, Upper Galwally, Belfast BT8 4TB tel 0232 491031

Livewire, Hawthorn House, Forth Banks, Newcastle upon Tyne NE1 3SG tel 091 261 5584

Made in Scotland Ltd, The Craft Centre, Station Road, Beauly, Invernesshire IV4 7EH tel 0463 782578. Marketing advice, group stands at trade fairs for craftspeople in Scotland.

Prince's Youth Business Trust (PYBT), 5 Cleveland Place, London SW1Y 6JJ tel 071 321 6500

Rural Development Commission, 141 Castle Street, Salisbury, Wiltshire SP1 3TP tel 0722 336255

Training and Enterprise Councils (TEC) Consult Yellow Pages or the Job Centre for your local TEC. TECs cover England and Wales; in Scotland similar organisations are called LECs.

Arts management training units

AMTIS (Arts Management Training Initiative Scotland), Chessels Land, Moray House Institute, Heriot Watt University, Edinburgh EH8 8AQ tel 031 558 6506

Arts Management Centre, Squires Building, University of Northumbria at Newcastle, Newcastle upon Tyne NE1 8ST tel 091 235 8933

Arts Training Programme, School of Performing Arts, De Montfort University, Leicester LE1 9BH tel 0533 577804

Arts Training South, Centre for Continuing Education, University of Sussex, Falmer, Brighton BN1 9RG tel 0273 606755

Centre for Arts Management, Institute of Public Administration and Management, University of Liverpool, 2 Abercromby Square, PO Box 147, Liverpool L69 3BX tel 051 794 2916

Regional Training Unit, South West Arts, 1 Constitution Hill, Bristol BS8 1DG tel 0272 253226

Professional organisations

Association for Applied Arts (AAA), c/o Ballantyne Mackay Associates, 2-8 Millar Crescent, Edinburgh EH10 5HW tel 031 447 9700. Represents Scottish makers, lobbying Government for support for applied arts in Scotland.

Association of Artists in Ireland (AAI), c/o Stella Coffey, Room 803, Liberty Hall, Dublin 1

Association of Illustrators, 29 Bedford Square, London WC1B 3EG tel 071 631 1510

Association of Photographers, 9/10 Domingo Street, London EC1Y OTA tel 071 608 1445

Autograph, 135 Bon Marché Building, 444 Brixton Road, London SW9 9NQ tel 071 274 4000. Association of black photographers.

AXIS: Visual Arts Information Service, Leeds Metropolitan University, Calverley Street, Leeds LS1 3HE tel 0532 833125. Registration forms available for the National Artists Register, a visual catalogue of work of artists, craftspeople and photographers in England, Scotland and Wales. Also developing UK Public Art Information Service.

British Artists in Glass, Broadfield House Glass Museum, Barnett Lane, Kingswinford, West Midlands DY6 9QA

British Toymakers Guild, 124 Walcot Street, Bath BA1 5BG tel 0225 442440

Chartered Society of Designers, 29 Bedford Square, London WC1B 3EG tel 071 631 1510

Craft Potters Association, William Blake House, 7 Marshall Street, London W1V 1FD tel 071 437 7605

Craftworks, 13 Linenhall Street, Belfast BT2 8AA tel 0232 236334. Membership organisation for craftspeople in Northern Ireland.

Design and Artists Copyright Society (DACS), St Mary's Clergy House, 2 Whitechurch Lane, London E1 7QR tel 071 247 1650

Federation of British Artists (FBA), 17 Carlton House Terrace, London SW1Y 5BD tel 071 930 6844. Umbrella organisation for nine different art societies including Royal Society of Portrait Painters, Society of Wildlife Artists, Royal Institute of Painters in Watercolours.

National Artists Association (NAA), Membership Secretary, 12 Brookside Terrace, Tunstall Road, Sunderland SR2 7RN

Printmakers Council (PMC), 31 Clerkenwell Close, London EC1R 0AT tel 071 250 1927

Regional craft guilds and potters associations: contact your local RAB or Crafts Council for details.

Rural Crafts Association, Heights Cottage, Brook Road, Wormley, Godalming, Surrey GU8 5UA tel 0428 682292

Society of Designer-Craftsmen, 24 Rivington Street, London EC2A 3DU tel 071 739 3663

Travel grants & charitable trusts

Arthur & Helen Davis Travelling Scholarship, The Clerk, Worshipful Company of Glaziers, Glaziers Hall, 9 Montague Close, London SE1 9DD tel 071 403 3300. Annual award (£1500) for a student or young artist in stained or decorative glass to travel to "widen their experience and develop their study and knowledge of glass".

David Canter Memorial Fund, The Secretary, PO Box 3, Ashburton, Devon TQ13 7UW. Annual awards of not less than £500 for craftspeople. Financial assistance for setting up, purchase of equipment, education, research, travel or special projects.

Partners in Europe (Go and See grants for under 26s), The Prince's Trust, 8 Bedford Row, London WC1R 4BA tel 071 405 5799

Winston Churchill Memorial Trust, 15 Queen's Gate Terrace, London SW7 5PR tel 071 584 9315

21 • Further reading

Selling and Marketing – general

Art, Design and Craft, A manual for business success, John Crowe & James Stokes, Edward Arnold, 1988, ISBN 0-7131-7514-1, £5.95. Useful book, especially for makers, with sound advice on marketing, commissions, insurance and finance.

Fact Pack 8: Art Materials and the Environment, Gary Roberts, AN Publications, £1.85 inc p&p. Information for environmentally conscious artists: suppliers and businesses promoting environmentally sound art and design.

Guide to Starting in Crafts, Angie & Paul Boyer, The Craftsman Magazine, 1991, ISBN 1-873847-00-9, £5.95 inc p&p. All you need to know about how to start in crafts and how to exhibit at craft fairs. Lots of practical information on doing markets and fairs.

Making Ways: The visual artists guide to surviving and thriving, Ed David Butler, AN Publications, 3rd ed, 1992, ISBN 0-907730-16-7, £11.99 plus £1 p&p. Comprehensive artists manual with sections on selling, exhibiting, commissions, insurance and keeping accounts.

Marketing for artists and craftspeople, Gerri Morris, North West Arts Board, 1993. Useful book with lots of examples of good practice which supports NWAB's training and advice initiatives for visual artists. Free from NWAB if you live in the region, contact them for price if you live elsewhere.

Marketing the visual arts, Arts Council of Great Britain, 1992, £20 plus £3.50 p&p. Practical manual on marketing and income generation for use by visual arts organisations. Positive advice on selling, creating the right opportunities for buying and customer care. From ACGB Marketing Department.

Organising Your Exhibition, Debbie Duffin, AN Publications, 2nd ed, 1991, ISBN 0-907730-14-0, £7.25 plus £1 p&p. Definitive guide for artists. Sections on finance, publicity, the private view and selling.

Running a Workshop: basic business for craftspeople, Ed Barclay Price, Crafts Council, 3rd ed, ISBN 1992, available from AN Publications at £7.75 plus £1 p&p. Essential sourcebook on setting up and running a craft workshop as a business. Sections on administration, costing, selling, exporting and publicity.

Seeing the Light: the photographer's guide to enterprise, Rhonda Wilson, Nottingham & Trent University, 1993, £11.60 inc p&p. Available from Dept of Photography, Nottingham & Trent University, Dryden Street, Nottingham tel 0602 418418.

Selling the Contemporary Visual Arts, Gerri Morris, Arts Council of Great Britain, 1992, £3.00. Marketing research report into markets and methods in the North West. From ACGB Marketing Department.

Southern Arts Resources Book, Anne Channon, Southern Arts, 1990, free to makers in SA region, £2.50 to others. Useful resources book for makers. Sections on finance, selling, publicity, export buying agencies, trade fairs, retail outlets, press contacts, photographers and postcard printers. Regional advisory listings but lots of information of use to visual artists everywhere. Due to be revised in 1993. From Southern Arts.

South East Arts Craft Resources Handbook, Anne Channon, South East Arts, 1992, free to makers in SEA region, £2.50 to others. Same model as above. Lots of useful information, not only for makers in the South East. From South East Arts.

The Fine Artist's Guide to Showing & Selling Your Work, Sally Prince Davis, North Light Books (USA), 1989, ISBN 0-89134-3083, £10.95. Practical advice American-style. Good guidance on gallery practice and contracts for selling in the USA.

The Greatest Little Business Book, Peter Hingston, Hingston, 5th ed, 1991, ISBN 0-906555-10-8, £6.95. Good general book, "the essential guide to starting a small business", on setting up and running a small business.

Working for Yourself in the Arts & Crafts, Sarah Hosking, Kogan Page, 2nd ed, 1989, ISBN 1-85091-717-5, £6.95. The artist as small business: sections on accounts, the product, marketing and selling and the market place.

Galleries and shops

Arts Review Yearbook, Arts Review, £13.95. Annual publication on "who's who and what's what in the art world". Listings of galleries, print publishers, auction houses, fine art magazines, arts festivals, art societies and suppliers of artists materials and services.

Directory of Exhibition Spaces, Ed Richard Padwick, AN Publications, 3rd ed, 1992, ISBN 0-907730-17-5, £13.99 plus £1 p&p. Comprehensive listing of over 2000 galleries in the UK and Ireland to help you find the right exhibition space.

Trade fairs and markets

Factpack 5: Craft Fairs, Kathryn Salomon, AN Publications, £1.85 inc p&p. Guide to the larger UK craft fairs plus national and international trade fairs. How to identify the right fair for you and organise for success.

The Craftworker's Year Book 1993, The Write Angle Press, ISBN 0-9520737-0-6, £9.50 inc p&p. 2000 craft fairs and marketing opportunities with details on costs and facilities, 200 craft event organisers, guilds, societies and publications. Published annually in two parts. Available from AN Publications.

Selling abroad

Across Europe, Ed David Butler, AN Publications, 1992, ISBN 0-907730-15-9, £9.95 plus £1 p&p. Exploration of travel and work in Europe. Inspiration from experiences of artists and makers in 24 countries. Contacts and information.

Europe: the Livewire Guide to Living and Working in the EC, Miranda Davies, Livewire Books for Teenagers/The Women's Press, ISBN 0-7-043-4949-9, 1992, £4.99. Thoroughly practical handbook with useful information for all ages on the other 11 EC countries.

Factpack 10: Travelling, Working & Selling in the EC, Emma Lister, AN Publications, £1.85 inc p&p. Opportunities, employment issues and reference section covering DTI foreign desks, cultural institutions, artists associations and copyright organisations in 12 EC countries.

Making Connections: the craftsperson's guide to Europe, Judith Staines, South West Arts, 1991, ISBN 0-9506991-9-5, £4.00 plus £1 p&p. Practical guide to marketing opportunities across Europe. Encourages networking through World Crafts Council Europe directory listing over 150 contacts. Available from AN Publications.

Financial and legal matters

Copyright, Roland Miller, ed David Butler, AN Publications, 1991, ISBN 0-907730-12-4, £7.25 plus £1 p&p. Guide for artists on how to use copyright to protect against exploitation: licences and contracts, fees and royalties.

Croners: series of standard reference works available in public libraries with current information on Business Information Sources, Employment legislation etc.

EEC Toy Safety Directive 1990: a guide to self-certification, British Toymakers Guild, £2.00 inc p&p. Available from British Toymakers Guild.

Fact Pack 1: Rates of Pay, Susan Jones, AN Publications, £1.85 inc p&p. Useful guide to establishing an hourly rate for commissions, workshops, talks etc.

Fact Pack 6: Insurance, Chris McCready, AN Publications, £1.85 inc p&p. Choosing the right insurance cover for your requirements and how to claim in the event of loss.

Health & Safety, Tim Challis & Gary Roberts, AN Publications, 1990, ISBN 0-907730-10-8, £7.25 plus £1 p&p. Required safety practices for artists and craftspeople.

Money Matters, Sarah Deeks, Richard Murphy & Sally Nolan, AN Publications, 1991, ISBN 0-907730-11-6, £7.25 plus £1 p&p. Essential financial information for all visual artists: VAT, customers, banks, suppliers, pricing work, keeping accounts.

Visual Arts Contracts, Nicholas Sharp, AN Publications, 1993, £3.50 each inc p&p. A unique series of sample contracts and agreements for artists, craftspeople, photographers and all others working in the visual arts.

Promotion

Fact Pack 2: Slide Indexes, Ed Susan Jones, AN Publications, £1.85 inc p&p. Lists over 40 artists indexes and slide registers.

Fact Pack 3: Mailing the Press, AN Publications, £1.85 inc p&p. How to publicise your work. List of press contacts including art magazines, general magazines, glossies, national press.

Fact Pack 4: Getting Media Coverage, Paul Gough, AN Publications, £1.85 inc p&p. How to get your work on radio and TV. Useful contacts list.

Illustration

Freelance Illustrator's Handbook, Carmel Hayes, Margaret Rose Press, ISBN 0-9518610-0-X, 1992, available from AN Publications £5.95 plus £1 p&p. Advice on getting work as an illustrator plus hundreds of contact names for illustrators, designers and artists.

Rights: the illustrator's guide to professional practice, Ed Simon Stern, Association of Illustrators, 1989, available from AN Publications £15.00 plus £1 p&p. Contracts, licences, fees, copyright, publishing, agencies.

Survive: the illustrator's guide to a professional career, Ed Aidan Walker, Association of Illustrators, 1989, available from AN Publications, £9.00 plus £1 p&p. Complete survival guide: presentation, agents, fees and listings.

Magazines

Art for Sale, Freepost 328, Bushey, Watford WD2 1FP tel 071 222 8866

Art Monthly, Suite 17, 26 Charing Cross Road, London WC2H 0DG tel 071 240 0389

Arts Review, 20 Prescott Place, London SW4 6BT tel 071 978 1000

Artist's and Illustrator's Magazine, Subscription Dept, Tower House, Sovereign Park, Market Harborough LE16 9EF tel 0858 46 8888

Artists Newsletter, PO Box 23, Sunderland SR4 6DG tel 091 514 3600

Ceramic Review, 21 Carnaby Street, London W1V 1PH tel 071 439 3377

Crafts, The Crafts Council, 44a Pentonville Road, London N1 9BY tel 071 278 7700

Craftsman Magazine, Subscriptions, 5 Lower Mead, Iver Heath, Bucks SL0 0DX tel 0753 817860

Maker's News, The Crafts Council (as for Crafts magazine). Distributed free to all makers on the Crafts Council Register.

22 • Glossary

Bad debt Person who owes you money, has defaulted for reasons of bankruptcy or dispute and where you know you will never get what is owed.

Cash on delivery Method of payment where by agreement a supplier of goods is paid on delivery. Payment can be by cash or cheque.

Commission (1) Also known as Mark-up or Percentage. The charge made by a selling outlet (shop or gallery) to the artist for their service in selling the work. Not to be confused with **Commission (2)**.

Commission (2) As in 'working to commission'. Producing work to an agreed brief, budget and specifications by arrangement with a private individual or public body, 'the commissioner'. Not to be confused with **Commission (1)**.

Consignment Also known as **Sale or Return**. Goods are deposited with a sales outlet (shop or gallery) agrees to sell them on your behalf. If unsold, the goods are returned or may be collected by the artist. Use a consignment contract/receipt to establish terms and conditions of sale and ownership of works.

Cost price Direct cost of making any item excluding profit. Often used (wrongly) to mean trade or wholesale price. See **Trade price**

Cost pricing Method of pricing which calculates the cost of materials, labour and overheads to price goods.

Credit terms Length of time given to a person or business to make payment for goods of services provided. Usually stated on the invoice as 'Terms: 30 days'.

Credit limit Largest single amount you can take as a credit card purchase before getting authorisation.

Direct cost Any costs directly attributable to making a piece of work. See **Overheads**.

Customs & Excise Government body which collects VAT and customs duties.

DTI Department of Trade and Industry. Government body which promotes export initiatives.

Enterprise Allowance Government-sponsored start-up scheme for small businesses, operated by the TECs. Scheme has different names in different areas, eg Business Start-Up, Business Boost, STEPS scheme. It pays accepted businesses between £20 – £90 per week for a period of 26-66 weeks. In some areas artists are not accepted onto the scheme.

Four Ps See **Marketing mix**

Invoice Document sent out by a person for services rendered or goods supplied stating details of goods or services and the cost.

LECs See **TECs**

Marketing mix Also known as the 'Four Ps'. The combining of product, price, place and promotion in different ways to appeal to different types of market.

Overheads Expenses incurred in running your business, eg studio rent, insurance, telephone.

Percentage See Commission

Profit Difference between your income and expenditure. If negative, it is called a loss.

Proforma Type of invoice giving details of goods or services to be supplied when payment received. It secures payment in advance of supply of goods.

PYBT The Prince's Youth Business Trust. Assistance for under 26s setting up in business.

RAB Regional arts boards – regionally established bodies in England which give support (including funding) to artists and craftspeople. In Wales, Scotland and Northern Ireland contact your arts council.

Reminder See **Statement**

Retail price Price at which work sells. In a gallery or shop this includes the commission plus VAT where appropriate.

Sale or return See **Consignment**

Selling price See **Retail price**

Statement Also known as a **Reminder**. Document giving details of an overdue payment for goods or services already supplied and invoiced. Not to be confused with Bank Statements.

TECs Training and Enterprise Councils, called LECs in Scotland. Local agencies which administer Enterprise Allowance scheme and offer business counselling and training advice.

Terms of trade Written statement as to the terms on which the supply of goods or services takes place.

Trade price Also known as Wholesale or (wrongly) as Cost price. The price placed on your work before an outlet's sales commission and VAT, where appropriate, are added. The amount the artist receives from a selling outlet for their work.

Value pricing Method of pricing which sets the price at what it is believed a customer will pay.

VAT Value Added Tax, a tax on certain goods and services, currently charged at between 0% and 17.5%. Known as TVA in some European countries.

Wholesale price See **Trade price**.

Index

Numbers in italics refer to page number of illustration
Entries in italics indicate titles of works

A

Adam, Jane, jeweller 8, 14, 29, *50,* 58, *85,* 91, 109
advertising 108; costs 75
agencies 74, 117
agents 67-70, 82; contracts 68, 93
Andersson, Jonathan, glassmaker 8, *32,* 34, 43, 47, 51
Art in Action 50
Art Boards 36
art collections (public and corporate) 77
ART 90 fair 47
art fairs 14, 46, 47, 52
artists' agents 69
'Artists Newsletter' 36, 46, 61, 77, 120
Artists Newsletter Information Service 67, 114
Artlink 38
art loan scheme 38
art markets 52-3
art purchase scheme 89
Arts Council (ACGB): grant for trade fairs 47; report 17, 19, 21, 38, 39, 52
Arts Councils 36, 121
Arts Management Centre 122
Arts Training Programme 122
Arts Training South 122
Art Supermarket 53
Artway 69
Assay Office 122
auctions 77
Autograph (Association of Black Photographers) 68, 122
AXIS Visual Arts Exchange and Information Service 74, 122

B

BANK *63*
banks, financial assistance 18, 27, 117-18
Barber, Louise *62*
Bateman, Roger, furniture maker 91-2, 114
Battersea Contemporary Art Fair 52
Beer, Vanilla, artist 12, 62-3, 73, *76*

Behennah, Dail, basket-maker *89*
Berg, Paul, furniture maker *80*
Blight, Victoria, stained glass artist *49*
Blue Cat Toy Company 50, 102, 106
Bourne, Sally, ceramicist 17, 105, 111
Bowen, Michelle, shop manager 28
Briscoe, Carlo, ceramicist *105*
British Council 121
British Toymakers Guild 102, 122
Business Design Centre, artMart 47
business enterprise agencies 117
buyers (purchasers) 19-21

C

Cassidy, Victoria, painter 12, *40,* 83
Centre for Arts Management 122
'Ceramic Review' 56, 82
ceramics and ceramicists 12, 13, *13,* 15, 17, 35, 44, 81, 105, *105;* auctions 77; directory 81; discounts 34; lead glazes 102; mail order 76; potters' associations 37, 122, 123; studio/workshop 54-5, *55,* 56; training 116
charitable trusts 120, 123
Chartered Society of Designers 122
Chelsea Crafts Fair 48, 69, 118
Christian, Yolanda, painter 77
Christmas, selling opportunities 16-17, 51, 55, 56, 75
Clarkson, Sheila, printmaker 12-13, 67
colleges 11, 12; pricing information 30; training 114
commissioned work 71-4; VAT charged on 86, 87
commission (mark-up) 28, 30, 31-2, 33-4, 42; agents 68, 69, 70; on exhibition sales 61, 62; on gallery sales 36, 38; on outright purchase 42; stated in contract 99; on studio sales 34
competitions 78
consignment *see* sale or return
Contemporary Art Society 53
Contemporary International Artists 62
contracts 43, 93-100; for commissioned work 73; gallery and artist (for VAT) 86; work cannot pass to a third party without artist's consent 92
copyright 97, 99, 102-3; for commissioned work 73
councils 69
Country Living Fair 46

craft agents 69
craft fairs 35, 42; contracts 95; listings 46; *see also* markets; trade fairs
Craft Potters Association 37, 122
'Crafts magazine' 36, 54, 56, 74, 120,
Crafts Council: address 121; computerised picture library 74; listings of trade fairs/markets 46; pre-fair seminar 48; selling overseas 79, 81; setting-up grants 14, 118; shops 36
'Crafts Council Map' 36, 37, 41
crafts and craftspeople 10, 16-17, 20; David Canter Memorial Fund 123; multimedia register 74
Crafts Potters Association Directory 81
'The Craftworker's Yearbook' 46
credit cards 39, 47, 76, 88
CVs 40, 41, 57, 61-2, 77, 104, 105, 106

D

Decorative and Applied Arts in Dorset 59
degree shows 42, 114
department stores 10, 39, 42; commission rate 32; mail order commissions 77; overseas buyers and agents 70, 81
Department of Trade and Industry (DTI) 122; advice on contacts overseas 70, 80; Export Development Advisers 113; grants or subsidies for international trade fairs 47, 81, 118, 119; 'New Products from Britain' scheme 81, 108
Design and Artists Copyright Society (DACS) 103, 123
directories 75
'The Directory of Exhibition Spaces' 36
Duffin, Debbie 62, 64
Dunkley, Sue, artist 44, *56,* 57, 64-5
Dunn, Edward, ceramicist *105*

E

Eastern Arts Board 121
East Midlands Arts (Board) 81, 115-16, 121
Edinburgh, Collective Gallery *37,* 46
Edmonds, Angela, artist 65, 90-1
electrical goods, safety 102
Enterprise Allowance scheme 18, 27, 115
European Community (EC): regulations 101, 102; VAT 87
European Textile Network 79
event listings 65, 108
exhibitions 10, 11, 16, 61-6; commission on sales 61, 62; contracts 93, 95; creating your own exhibition space 63, *63;* group initiatives 57, 64, 66; hired space 62-3; innovative approach to selling *37;* 'mark of quality' 30; organising your own 62-6; private view 62, 66; publicity/promotion 64-6; in shopping malls 14, 63; talks by artist 108-9; where to find listings 36
Export Buying Offices Association (EXBO) 81, 122
exports *see* overseas

F

Federation of British Artists 73, 123
financial assistance (grants, subsidies) 117-20; applying 16; groups 64; for selling abroad 47, 80-1, 118, 119; to help with exhibition 57; for trade fairs 47-8, 117
fine artists 10, 31, 34, 43
Foster, Tony, artist *31*
Francis, Mike, ceramicist 46
Frannie, designer-maker 28, 42, 76-7, *113*
Friends of the Earth 76
Funnell, Christian 70, 73

G

galleries 11, 14, 22, 36-45; advice from 43-4; advisory service for buyers 20; assessing success 39-40; buyers from 42; chasing debts 89, 90; commission/mark-up 31-2, 36, 42; creating own exhibition space 63; direct contact with artist 68, 69; discounts 34; exhibition publicity/promotion 64-5; how to approach 41-2; overseas 81; pricing 30, 44; private and 'commercial' 36, 37-8; producing work for 44; public/subsidised 36, 38-9; and purchasers 21; sale or return 32, 43, 95, 98-9; special purchase schemes 89; trade price 30, 31; undercutting their prices not advised 34, 54; VAT 84-7; work bought by public collection 77
Gateshead, Portcullis Gallery 35
glass 20, 32, 35, *81;* Arthur & Helen Davis Travelling Scholarship 123; British Artists in Glass 122; exporting overseas 34-5; price labelling 35
grants *see* financial assistance
Greenpeace 76
Gregory, Caroline Bousfield, potter 54-5
groups: stand at trade fairs 47; studios and exhibitions 56-7, 64, 66
'The Guardian, Art for Sale' 75

H

Hall, Diane, jeweller 79
Hawkins, James, painter 54
Hayes, Carmel, illustrator 70
house sales 14, 54-6; insurance 58, 91; marketing 60; permission to trade 58; planning consent 58; promotion 60; rates 58-9; security 59; use retail prices 54
Humphreys, Mel 11-12

I

illustrators: agents 70; Association of Illustrators 122; further reading 126; training 116
insurance 58, 91-2; and agents 68; mail order 75
International Ceramics Academy 80
Ireland: Arts Councils 121; Association of Artists in Ireland 122; Crafts Council 80, 121
Irwin, Bernard *13*

Index

J

James, Shani Rhys, artist *26*
jewellery and jewellers *50;* at trade fairs 51; discounts 34; hallmarking legislation 102
Just, Erica, textile artist *16,* 81

L

law *see* legislation
Law, Frances, artist 8
Lawrence, Deborah, photographer *107*
Leach, John, potter 8, 13, *55,* 56
legislation 101-3
Lewis, Mark, sculptural furniture designer *78*
Liberty's, British Crafts Room 39
Livewire 112, 119, 122
local authorities, grants 80, 119
London Arts Board 121
London Enterprise Agency 115
Loydell, Rupert, artist 30

M

magazines: further reading 126; publicity through features 106-7; selling through 75
mailing list 42, 51, 62, 64, 66, 110
mail order selling 75-7, 106
Makers Guild 37
Manchester Festival 53
marketing 15-17, 18-24; attracting attention of shop buyers and dealers 42; courses 116; exhibitions 64-6; four 'Ps' (action plan) 23; grants to employ a consultant 119; reviewing 111-13; SMART objectives 22, 112; SWOT analysis 18-19, 22, 24, 112
markets 51-2, 53; costs 47-8; listings 46; payment at 88; preparation for 48; publicity 48; retail price 34; *see also* trade fairs
media 65, 78, 106-8
Munroe, Keith, potter 48
museums 38, 69; contracts 93

N

National Artists Association 123
National Trust 76
New Academy Gallery 30
Newell, Eleanor 12
Northern Arts Board 121; Art Purchase Plan 89
Northern Ireland: Arts Councils 118, 121; Craftworks 123; LEDU 116, 122
North West Arts Board 121

O

The Omnibus Survey 20
open studios 56-7, 60
outlets 14, 24, 67; advantages and disadvantages 45; advice from 43-4; assessing their success in selling work 39-40; collecting debts 89-90; how to approach 41-2; mark-up/commission 28, 33; outright purchase 42-3; sale or return 42, 43;

special purchase schemes 89; *see also* art fairs; art markets; Art Supermarket; auctions; competitions; department stores; exhibitions; galleries; museums; shopping malls; shops; overseas
overseas 79-82; agents 70, 81, 82; collecting debts 92; export price lists 34-5; financial assistance 47, 80-1, 119; payment methods 84; press coverage 108; trade fairs 79, 81, 118, 119; translate instructions for assembly or use 101; VAT 82, 87

P

packaging 44, 57
painters and paintings 16, 44; studio/gallery 54
payment 88, proforma 34, 42, 43, 90; *see also* credit cards
Penn-Smith, Sally, glass designer 20, 24, 35, 47, *81,* 115
Petherick, Ann, art adviser *20,* 41
photography/photographers *107;* agents for 70; Association of Photographers 122; multimedia register 74; *see also* Autograph
Pieroni, Leonardo 56
Pollock, Polly, basket-maker 61, 72
presentation, framing and packaging 44
pricing 15, 17, 23, 25-35; advice from outlet 44; calculate costs (cost-pricing) 26-8; a commissioned work 73, 74; discounts 34; export price lists 34-5; fair/market 47, 52; gallery 34; hourly rates 27; reviewing 112; selling from house/studio 54; trade and retail prices 28, 30, 31-2, 33-4, 42, 43, 49-50, 54; value-pricing 25-6, 29-30
Prince's Trust 78, 122; Go & See grant 81, 119; Partners in Europe 119, 123
Prince's Youth Business Trust 47, 112-13, 118-19
printmakers (and prints) 20, 21, 33, 34, 38-9; craft outlets 32; Printmakers Council 123; selling in department stores 39; selling through mail order 75
promotion/publicity 23, 104-10; for commissioned work 74; for exhibitions 64-6; further reading 126; reviewing 112; for selling from home/studio 57, *59,* 60; through competitions 78; for trade fairs and markets 48; *see also* media

R

Regional arts boards (RABs) 46, 47, 67, 81, 115-16, 118
Regional Training Unit 122
regulations *see* legislation
reviewing progress 111-13
road signs 60
Rodrigues, Teresa 52
Rookledge, Gavin, book artist *69,* 106
Rural Crafts Association 46, 123
Rural Development Commission (RDC) 60, 80; address 122; financial assistance 119; marketing courses 116

S

safety 101; selling from studio 57, 58; of toys 101-2

sale or return (consignment) 32, 42, 43, 45, 83, 84, 86; abroad 81-2; contract to use 95, 98-9; if gallery goes bust 90

sales administration 83-92; chasing debts 89-91; getting paid 88-9; keeping records 83-4; legal action 90-1; *see also* VAT

sales legislation *see* legislation

sales package 41-2, 83

Saltsman, Avis *21*

Scotland: AMTIS 122; Association for Applied Arts 122; AXIS multimedia register 74, 122; grants 48; Made in Scotland 122; Scottish Arts Council 118, 121; Scottish Enterprise 116

security 51, 59

Sellars, Julie, jeweller 41

shopping malls, exhibition space 14, 63

shops 14, 36-45; advice from 43-4; assessing success 39-40; buyers from 42; commission/mark-up 31, 32, 42; contracts 93, 95, 98-9; contracts with dealer 95; craft and fine art 36-7; direct contact with artist 68, 69; how to approach 41-2; price 44; producing work for 44; sale or return 42, 43, 95, 98-9; special purchase schemes 89; trade price 30, 31, 33; undercutting their prices not advised 34, 54; VAT 31, 84-6; *see also* department stores

Sight Specific 74

slide registers and indexes 68, 69, 74, 118; copyright symbol 103

Society of Designer-Craftsmen 72, 123

Soden, Robert, artist *72*

South East Arts (Board) 77, 118, 121

Southern Arts Board 59, 121

South West Arts Board 59, 121

'start-up' schemes 27; *see also* financial assistance

Stockport Art Gallery, Artlink 38

studio sales 14, 44, 54-6; charge retail price 34; contracts 95; insurance 58, 91; marketing 60; open studios 56-7, 60; payment methods 57; permission to trade 58; planning consent 58; promotion 60; regulations 58-9; security 59

T

talks and demonstrations 16, 108-9

TECs *see* Training and Enterprise Councils

textiles and textile artists *16,* 28, 68, 101, *113;* painted clothes 10, *29*

Thorn, Josephine *9*

Toms, Anne 71

Tourist Board 60

toys 101-2; British Toymakers Guild 102, 122

trade fairs 48-51, 53; buyers visiting 106; costs 47-8; display 49-50; financial assistance 47, 117; foreign buyers 79; insurance 91; listings 46; overseas 81, 118, 119; payment (cash/cheques) 88; preparation 48; promotion/publicity 46-7, 48; records of orders 84; retail price 34; sales technique 50-1; security 51; trade buyers 49, 50

trade marks 103

training 18, 114-16; art and design colleges 114; arts management organisations 115-16; enterprise programmes 115

Training and Enterprise Councils (TECs) 80, 115, 122

travel grants 81, 117, 123

U

USA: consumer protection advice 101; mail order 76-7; poison in ceramic glazes 102

V

VAT 28, 30, 31, 84-7, 96, 97, 98, 99; selling abroad 82

W

Wales: AXIS multimedia register 74, 122; Collectorplan 89; listings of outlets 36; Welsh Arts Council 118, 121; Welsh Development Agency 116

Waller, Carole, painter 10, *29,* 56, 104-5

Warner, Tony 47

Warsop, Anna, painter/printmaker 8, 26, 30, 44, *109*

Westley, Michael 56

West Midlands Arts Board 121

Willis, Lucy, painter 8, *11,* 73, 78

Winston Churchill Memorial Trust 120, 123

Y

York, Kentmere House Gallery *20*

Yorkshire and Humberside Arts Board 121

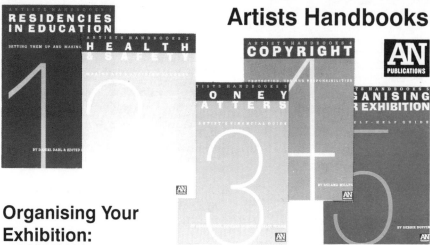

Artists Handbooks

Organising Your Exhibition:
the self-help guide
Debbie Duffin

"A do-it-yourself guide designed to help... artists to get their work on the wall with the minimum of agony." Wideangle

"...detailed advice on pitfalls ranging from dealing with printers to buying wine." Art Monthly

The revised and updated edition of Debbie Duffin's invaluable practical guide offers excellent advice on finding space, finances, publicity, insurance, framing and hanging work, private views and selling. The essential sourcebook on setting up and running any exhibition.
116 pages £7.25 + £1 p&p

Copyright:
protection, use &responsibilities
Roland Miller

"...a comprehensive guide." Portfolio Magazine

Essential advice on negotiating rewarding copyright agreements; exploiting the earning and promotional potential of copyright; and dealing with infringement of copyright. Designed to help *you* make the most of copyright.
128 pages, illustrated £7.25 + £1 p&p

Health & Safety:
making art & avoiding dangers
Tim Challis & Gary Roberts

"It is in the interest of all artists to study the contents of this handbook." Leisure Painter

Making art can be dangerous. Artists and makers now use substances and processes which can damage human health and the environment. This unique handbook covers all art and craft forms to help you protect people and the environment, and prepare your COSHH assessment.
144 pages, illustrated £7.25 + £1 p&p

Money Matters:
the artist's financial guide
Sarah Deeks, Richard Murphy & Sally Nolan

"...recommended." Ceramic Review

Reliable user-friendly advice on: tax, National Insurance, VAT, keeping accounts, pricing your work, grants, insurance, dealing with customers, suppliers and banks, and much more. Features an accounting system specially devised for artists.
134 pages, illustrated £7.25 + £1 p&p

Residencies in Education Daniel Dahl

Essential for everyone interested in understanding the role and responsibilities of artists in schools. It explores the relationship between project, artist and teachers, and covers contracts and payments, funding training. Useful information and further reading sections.
124pp, illustrated £7.25 + £1 p&p

AN Publications, PO Box 23, Sunderland SR4 6DG. Tel 091 514 3600, Fax 091 564 1600
Prices quoted are the prices in force as of May 1993 and are subject to change.

135

Artists Handbooks

Art in Public
What, Why and How
ed Susan Jones

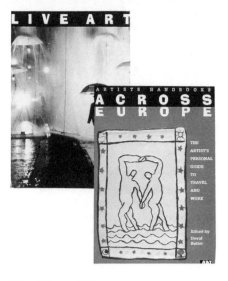

"It covers much of the ground which needs to be discussed, debated and evaluated 'in the field' and in education"
Faye Carey, Chelsea College of Art and Design

A highly recommended and essential discourse on the application of artwork to environmental and architectural sites, spaces and surfaces. Draws on first hand practical experiences and covers commissions, time-scales, funding, site for work, practical considerations for writing and presenting proposals and making applications.
178pp, illustrated £9.95 + £1 p&p

Directory of Exhibition Spaces 93/94
(3rd edition) ed Richard Padwick

"No self-respecting artist who wants to show and sell work should be without it."
Working for Yourself in the Arts and Crafts

A comprehensive listing of over 2000 galleries in the UK and Eire to help you find the right exhibition space. Details who to apply to, type of work shown, space and facilities. An unrivalled visual arts reference resource with an impressive track record, now published biennially
256 pages, illustrated £13.99 + £1 p&p

Across Europe:
the artist's personal guide to travel and work
ed David Butler

"... a much needed sourcebook."
Sam Yates, Crafts Council Bookshop

A combination of artists' first-hand experiences and hard facts gets under the Eurospeak to show what '1992-and-all-that' could mean for you. Over 20 European nations are covered, giving information on: organisations, funding, magazines, agencies and other sources of information. A must for everyone interested in selling, exhibiting, working or training in Europe.
168 pages, illustrated £9.95 + £1 p&p

Making Ways:
the artist's guide to surviving and thriving
3rd edition, ed David Butler

"...a thorough and thoughtful compilation of fact, theory and practicle example... a vital part of every visual and applied artist's survival kit."
Gail Boardman, Craftwork

New edition of the visual artist's professional bible, revised and brought bang up-to-date to help you 'survive and thrive' in the '90s. Features important new sections on selling, presentation and opportunities abroad. Everything you need to know about the 'business end' of being an artist.
288 pages, illustrated £11.99 + £1 p&p

Live Art
ed Robert Ayers & David Butler
"an inspiration" Live Art Listings

What is live art? How far does it overlap and integrate with other art forms? However you define your art, if it involves live or non-permanent elements this book is for you. It includes advice on putting a performance together, touring work, copyright, contracts and documentation, with examples of live art through photographs and comments by artists. For everyone who wants to develop, earn from, or promote live art.
178 pages, illustrated £7.95 + £1 p&p

AN Publications, PO Box 23, Sunderland SR4 6DG. Tel 091 514 3600, Fax 091 564 1600
Prices quoted are the prices in force as of May 1993 and are subject to change.